COUNT IT ALL JOY

A child with a handicap is sometimes referred to as 'a trial'. On the contrary, we have found that James has brought into our lives, and into the lives of other people who know him, enrichment and joy.

COUNT IT ALL JOY

Betty McKay

Christian Focus Publications

© 1992 Betty McKay
ISBN 1 871 676 866

Published by
Christian Focus Publications Ltd
Geanies House, Fearn, Ross-shire,
IV20 1TW, Scotland, Great Britain.

Printed and bound in Great Britain by
Cox & Wyman Ltd, Reading

Cover photograph
by
D&B Photography, Stonehaven

Cover design
by
Seoris N. McGillivray.

Contents

My Thanks To:

Paul, Moira, Maureen and Elaine - for their help and technology
David - for constant support and encourage-ment
James - for just being himself

Diagnosis

James was a chubby two-year-old with straight, very blond hair and deep set, trusting grey-green eyes. He smiled as he sat on the soft, living-room carpet holding up a yellow plastic toy to the tall stranger who was visiting.

"Duck!" he said invitingly. "Duck!"

The man made no response. He was a child psychologist and his brief visit was nearly over. Ignoring the little boy he turned to me. "He's ineducable," he said shortly, and started towards the door.

In a daze I followed him and showed him out. That tiny sentence seemed to have numbed my senses, leaving the one terrible word 'ineducable' to burn itself into my brain.

Seconds later the door closed behind him and I went back into the living room where James was still contentedly playing.

Suddenly I was glad to sit down and try to recover from the body blow of those awful words. Just what did they mean for James? For all of us?

"Count it all joy, my brethren, when you meet various trials..."   James 1:2 RSV

CHAPTER ONE

Early Days

I was born in Golcar, a village in the Colne Valley not far from Huddersfield in Yorkshire. Like most members of my family, I had worked in the woollen textile trade until I married. David was born in Montrose, Scotland, his parents being natives of the nearby town of Forfar. When he was a little over a year old they had moved to northern England. Work was scarce in the early thirties but, as a research chemist, David's father had found a job with ICI, so he and his wife and young baby had moved south and eventually settled in Huddersfield.

David and I met when our respective mothers, who did not know each other, encouraged us to join a newly formed Youth Choir. (It can pay to obey your parents!) We had plenty of time to become acquainted during the six years of David's training to be a dental surgeon.

We married in 1954 and our first son, Paul, was born in Huddersfield in March 1955. We were living with my parents temporarily because David was still at Leeds University studying for a further degree and his own parents had moved back to Scotland due to David's father's deteriorating health.

In 1956 David achieved his B.Ch.D and then had to fulfil his deferred obligation to the Crown and do National Service. He opted to serve in the RAF as a dentist. With his qualification he was obliged to become an officer, though starting at the lowest rank. At that time, officers below the age of 25 were not paid a marriage allowance while doing National Service. By agreeing to serve for three years instead of two, David obtained slightly better terms, which gave us just enough to live on.

After two weeks of initial training he got a weekend pass and came to visit us.

"I've been posted to Ballykelly," he said.

"Northern Ireland?" I guessed, though I'd never heard of the actual place. I was later to discover Ballykelly to be typical of the many roadside villages in that part of the world - a scattering of houses, a pub or two, a church, an Orange Hall - all set in lush green countryside. The RAF camp had some but not enough married quarters, so many of the regular officers as well as the National Service-men found accommodation wherever they could, within a twenty mile radius.

As soon as David arrived he started to scout

around for a place for us to live. He spent his first Saturday with Stewart Moorhead, the house agent in Castlerock. A few days later he was able to write and tell me that he had found rooms for us there. We were to join him as soon as possible.

Two weeks passed before David could return to the Colne Valley. That weekend we loaded all our worldly goods into our little maroon Morris van - baby's bath, blankets, crockery, folding pram, electric iron - everything was packed in until the poor van would not have held another coat hanger! Then David drove it alone on the old, pre-motorway roads to Stranraer and from there crossed to Northern Ireland. Paul and I followed by air four days later.

Even as a child I knew that I didn't want to live permanently in the Colne Valley and I looked forward to being all together again in a new environment away from the industrial grime which I had always found depressing.

We had to spend the first weekend in lodgings in Limavady, the nearest town to Ballykelly, because our rooms in Castlerock were not quite ready. So it was there that we had our first taste of culture shock.

Our bedroom was over a corner shop - the kind which, like so many in Northern Ireland, stays open all hours. Our meals were served in a dining room behind the shop. The room was so dark that one's

11

eyes were immediately drawn to the small, bright square of window set high in a corner of the wall.

Two things struck me at our first teatime meal. No fewer than seven different kinds of bread were set out on the table. By trial and error -and some surreptitious passing on to David - I discovered that most of them contained baking soda - a taste to be acquired, but not on that first day.

The second unusual element was seeing several black-coated policemen (I later learned they were called 'B' Specials) join us at the table. As they entered the room they casually removed the bullets from their revolvers, and hung the bandoliers on a coat stand in the corner. When they had eaten and were ready to leave, they re-loaded.

More culture shock followed later in the evening. I was trying, without much success, to settle Paul to sleep in a strange cot. Several times his eyes were just closing when the sound of loud drums and flutes or accordions jerked him back to full consciousness. I was exasperated and went to the window to see what was going on. In the street down below a band of twenty kilted pipers skirled lustily.

It transpired that our room was on the route for a rehearsal for the Orangemen's Day parade to be held on the Twelfth of July. The bands from all the town's Lodges would be marching round and round the block of four streets for the whole evening!

We knew when we were beat. We lifted Paul and joined the rest of the world outside. With the baby in his pram we sauntered along the crowded pavements in the warm evening air, amazed to see so many children and tiny tots, who by our English standards should have been fast asleep in bed.

I shall never forget my first experience of Castlerock. David drove us there over the mountain road so that we saw it at first from a height - a pale arc of sand bisected by a pier where the River Bann flowed into the sea. David drove us right down to sea level and parked at the road's end. It was a fine June day, the sea sparkling in the sunlight on an almost deserted beach. The contrast to my lifelong experience of the soot-blackened industrial Yorkshire environment could not have been more complete.

"Oh yes," I breathed, "I shall love it here. I don't want to go anywhere else."

The rooms we had booked were in Kengate, a two-storeyed house at the crossroads of the village. The other occupants of the house were door-to-door salesman Robin, his wife Gwen, their baby daughter Ruth, Robin's brother, Herbert - a devotee of early morning reheated tea left over from the night before - Gwen's mother, Mrs. Eakin from Limerick, three cats, which had to be kept inside, and a dog which had to be kept out!

Their main contribution to our culture shock was their daily habit of boiling a huge enamel pot of unpeeled potatoes and setting it, drained, on the table to be shared amongst the four of them for their evening meal. Spearing a potato with a fork, they deftly removed the skin with a knife, anointed it with butter and salt and washed it all down with plenty of milk. Sometimes they would have a small tin of sardines as relish, followed by strong tea.

Even though we shared the kitchen I was glad we were to do our own catering! No doubt they were equally amazed - and perhaps amused - to see me making steamed chocolate pudding and custard almost daily for part of Paul's lunch. No doubt they thought I was into *in*convenience foods, but Paul loved it.

By the end of August the few summer visitors to Castlerock had all departed and from the first of September Mr. Moorhead was able to offer us a furnished house of our own, set in a sloping garden overlooking the sea. All this for a rent of twelve pounds a month.

A few miles from the mouth of Lough Foyle on the north coast of Ireland, Castlerock consisted of a scattering of tall, blackstone houses which lined the coast as far as the cliffs would allow, while others trailed back into the green hills rising gently beyond. Two churches, one Presbyterian and the other Church of Ireland, stood like parentheses at each end of the village, enclosing two hotels, a Post Office, a railway station and a few very basic shops. There were about 300 inhabitants, many of them retired, elderly people along with a few, frequently-changing RAF families. It seemed to us to be an ideal place to live.

While David was at Ballykelly every day, Paul and I enjoyed together the freedom of the beach at the bottom of the garden. I soon discovered that it was never enough to take a bucket and spade with us when we went there. These palled after a very few minutes and Paul would rummage in my bag for the book he knew he would find there. We spent hours in the lee of a rock or in the shelter of a sand dune, leafing through the pages of his book, naming flowers, birds, boats and a variety of people and toys.

In the summer of 1957 Helen was born. Some of the local folk, and even our own letter-writing relatives, wondered if Paul would be jealous.

But with two-and-a-half year old wisdom he explained quite simply to a lady who was inspecting the new occupant of the pram: "She's Mummy's baby. I'm Daddy's boy." And indeed he was. When he woke in the night, as he sometimes did, it was no good my going to him.

"Daddy! Daddy!" he would cry, shying away from me. So Daddy would have to go to see to 'his' boy.

When Helen was one month old we moved a little further along and across the road into a house of our own called Rossdowney. Our friend Mr. Moorhead had pointed out that, for ten shillings a month less, we could be buying our own house rather than paying rent. Then, if we decided to move when David's term of service was over, we would have something to sell.

Somehow we managed to scrape together enough savings for a deposit and bought our first house. A typical three bed-roomed semi, it had a garden back and front and a driveway wide enough for a garage which we later built, flanking the sunny end of it with a lean-to greenhouse. By September we were living in our very own house!

Two years later, in the summer of 1959, David completed his National Service and in November, our third baby, James, was born.

As the three years of daily driving over the mountains, or via the coast road to Ballykelly drew to a close, we had to ask ourselves: What next? Perhaps where next? Should David look for a dental job locally so that we could stay in Northern Ireland, or should we sell our house and move back across the water?

It wasn't a hard decision to make. By then we were so well used to the Irish pace of life that we had no wish to leave. I had even started buying buttermilk by the quart to make my own soda bread! And we still loved Castlerock.

There might not be many shops, but the grocer sent round a young boy each morning to take any orders and he delivered them later. A selection of butcher's vans came round, at least one every day except Sunday, and Liptons van brought us cut price goods once a week. Supermarkets might not exist, but we didn't need them.

Personally I found it far easier to shop literally on my own doorstep than to get the children togged up and trail them around the shops. All in all the lifestyle suited us well. So when a School Dental job was advertised, based in Ballymoney, David applied for and got it. From June onwards he travelled thirteen miles east to his base clinic, though his area of schools covered a large part of North Antrim. He was well installed in the job by November when James was due.

Before Paul was born I'd had toxaemia and he was induced early. Again with James my blood pressure rose alarmingly towards the end of my pregnancy and I had to go into the Maternity Home about a week before the baby was due so that I could have complete rest.

On Saturday evening during visiting hours, I felt the early stages of labour begin. I rang for the nurse.

"You'll be a wee while yet, darlin'," she said cheerily. "We'll move you along to the Labour Ward when visiting time's over."

But it was only a few minutes later that James made a swift entry into the world in the presence of his father!

The ironic thing was that, when we had asked about it earlier, we had been refused permission for David to be present at the birth. Such things were not allowed in Northern Ireland in the fifties. Though we were unconscious of it at the time, God granted our request!

My mother travelled over from Yorkshire to help with the children and we soon adjusted our family routine to include our new baby boy.

Right from the start James seemed to be an unusually good baby. He rarely cried. It was true that he took ages to de-wind, and quite often regurgitated breast milk down his nose which made it difficult for him to breathe, but once he was soundly asleep he would stay that way for hours. Much longer than my neighbour's baby of the same age. Sometimes James only woke for a feed twice in twenty four hours!

Following tradition we had him christened in the Presbyterian church where Paul was attending Sunday School. We chose the names James Strang because it was very much a McKay family name - James has an uncle, a great-uncle and a great-grandfather with the same names.

I didn't have any friends really because we no longer had RAF contacts and the families we had known had moved away but the children kept me fully occupied and I never felt lonely.

David was usually home by 4pm and he took over the children while I made our evening meal. After that he would bath them and put them to bed. We had become accepted as residents and people greeted us on the street, even though few invited us into their homes. I was happy with things as they were.

Life at that time was pleasantly busy. Paul was four and a half and had started school. I took him along to catch the school bus each morning because the school was almost a mile out in the country. I would have James in the big, black coachbuilt pram which we had bought second-hand for him, and Helen would either be perched on the apron or trotting beside us.

At this time too we acquired our one and only dog, Paddy. He was a fragile-looking, fawn whippet, and the gentlest of creatures.

"Why did you want to buy a whippet?" the village policeman asked when he saw David out with the dog. ''The law says they've to be on a lead and muzzled at all times when they're out.''

As Paddy was not even keen on wearing a collar let alone a lead and a muzzle, it sometimes took me as long to get him ready for the road as the children! But we managed.

It was at this time too that a long suppressed desire to write overcame me. I saw an advertisement for a writing course which promised a money-back guarantee to all who had not earned the cost of the course by the time they completed the assignments. I never actually did complete the course - though I did manage to sell two short stories which covered my expenses.

I well remember writing the rough pencil draft of the first assignment sitting up in bed in the middle of the night with James over my left shoulder waiting for his feed to settle comfortably. I wrote thousands of words in the undisturbed quietness of those middle-of-the-night sessions with James.

With hindsight I can see that he was perhaps a slow baby in many ways, but at the time I accepted it as being just part of his personality. He was seventeen months old before he could walk and inevitably I compared him with Paul and Helen. They had both been well on their feet by the time they were a year old.

He didn't speak as early as they had either, and the funny thing was that he spoke when *he* wanted to rather than on demand.

We had a rose pink geranium on a window ledge at a turn of the stair and when I carried him past it in the morning he would point one fat finger skyward and say ''F'ower''.

''Yes, that's a flower!'' I'd say, delighted. ''Say it again, James. Say flower.''

But he would look at me in a puzzled way as we went on down the stairs. There was no longer any flower in sight. So why say 'flower'? And he wouldn't!

It was his Granny, my mother-in-law, who first made open comment about him confirming my own suspicions. She and Grandpa were over from Scotland on their annual spring visit and one morning she was pushing him gently in a swing which we had suspended in the kitchen doorway. James was chuckling with pleasure.

''There's something just not quite right about James,'' she said. ''I'd ask the doctor about him if I were you.''

I didn't argue. Perhaps because she saw the children only at intervals she was able to spot things that I might not notice. So on our next visit to the surgery I asked about James' slowness.

''There's nothing to worry about,'' the doctor

assured me. "You can't expect everybody to be as bright as your Paul and Helen. Just wait, James'll be fine."

So I pushed my uneasiness away and allowed myself to be reassured. It was true that all children varied in their progress and as long as he got there in the end, why worry? Besides, there would soon be another baby on the scene.

Alison arrived in March 1962 when James was almost two and a half and he soon became her devoted admirer and my official 'helper'.

He would pass me fresh nappies or sprinkle powder on to the new baby, obviously happy to do his bit. I accepted his help as much as I could, to encourage him. But I always felt I had to be watchful, just in case. In spite of my caution he once tipped the whole pram right over when he was climbing up to see if the baby was still asleep! Fortunately it was indoors and although they all landed on the floor, no harm was done. In fact I learned to work in the kitchen with the pram wedged in the doorway so I could keep my eye on them both.

James loved washdays. I had a big, square washing machine with powered wringers and James used to sit on a stool beside it. I sometimes left the lid off so that he could watch the white, soapy bubbles frothing about as the clothes swirled round and round. Perhaps it was inevitable, but one day when my back was turned, he stood up, leaned over and fell into the hot suds head first!

I grabbed the back of his orange woollen coat and hauled him out gasping, mercifully unhurt - and very clean! Later on that day he developed two dark purple bruises where the agitator had hit his temples.

And that wasn't James' only accident in the kitchen.

Sometimes he would stand up in his wooden high chair when we were having a meal and, without warning and before either of us could grab him, he would fall down on to the red tiled floor. He sported many a purple lump on his forehead!

Then one day when we were out for a walk, a car drew up beside the pram. It was the District Nurse.

"I called at the house but you were out," she said. "I'll come back later - unless there's anything special?"

Suddenly I found myself telling her of my suspicions about James. I asked her what she thought.

"Would you like the child psychologist to call and see him?" she offered. "He'll tell you better than I could. He'll come to the house."

So he did. He paid us that one brief visit. Without giving James any kind of test or even speaking to him, he pronounced the verdict that upset me so much: Ineducable. At first I was completely stunned. And at that time I didn't realise that God might have any plan or purpose for our situation. I had only had a real relationship with him for a few months.

~~~~~~

We were never given a precise diagnosis of James' condition at any one time, but we understand that brain damage had probably been caused by lack of oxygen in the last few weeks before he was born. He is slow and slightly spastic and has an IQ of about 68.

~~~~~~

CHAPTER 2

A Glimmer of Hope

As a child I'd been sent to a Methodist Sunday School - twice every Sunday. Then I'd graduated to teaching in that same Sunday School and I also sang in the chapel choir. If anyone had asked me if I were a Christian I'd have said 'Yes', believing it to be true.

In fact it wasn't until we were married and had moved to Northern Ireland that Willie Norwell, an elderly Irish farmer, happened to be visiting David on business and began to talk about Jesus, first to David and then to both of us.

Sitting in a corner chair by the open fire one cold November evening, Willie drew a well worn black Bible from his jacket pocket and talked to us about Christ. He spoke as if he knew him. I was fascinated! I had gone to Sunday School and chapel all those years and yet it seemed that nobody had ever really told me anything like this before. He said that everybody - including me - needed to be saved by God's grace. It wasn't enough just to know *about*

Jesus. I needed to respond to his love by asking him into my life as Saviour and Lord. To hand my life completely over to him.

"But why didn't anybody tell me all this before?" I asked. "Which church do you belong to?"

"It isn't belonging to any church that'll save you," Willie said, wisely not revealing his denomination, though we later found it to be Open Brethren. "It's whether or not you belong to Jesus that counts."

I knew at once that I wanted very much to belong to Jesus; to have a real relationship with him myself so that, when I died, I would go to be with him forever as Willie had read from his battered old Bible. David felt the same and later, each on our own, we both asked Jesus into our lives.

We started to attend the Presbyterian Church in Castlerock though we rarely managed to get there together as they had no creche. After a while David started to teach a Sunday School class in the morning and he allowed me to escape the family bedtime routine and enjoy the peacefulness of the evening service.

Another person who helped me greatly was an older lady who lived with her sisters across the street. Somehow she heard about our new commitment to Christ and came across to visit us. Miss Mary Pollock already knew Paul and Helen because they were in her Primary Sunday School class, so we had a ready-made talking point.

As we chatted I learned that she was deeply interested in missionary work in many parts of the world. As time went on she introduced me to missionaries from Africa, Nepal and India when they came to stay with her and she also passed on missionary magazines and letters for me to read. It was all grist to the mill and it was due to her influence that I assumed that every Christian had an automatic interest in world mission.

One summer Sunday evening she took me to the Portstewart Keswick Convention. It was my first experience of standing in a huge wind-wafted marquee with hundreds of Christians praising God together. And it opened up a whole new dimension for me.

On a less exotic level, she gave me Scripture Union Bible reading notes and encouraged me to start to read and pray every day - no small feat with four children under seven!

These notes were just what I needed, though I'm sure I didn't recognise it at the time. In spite of my Sunday School days - even, I began to think with horror, my Sunday School *teaching* days! - my Bible knowledge was virtually nil. I needed to develop a steady, day-by-day habit of reading God's Word. But I also needed the guidance and teaching of those explanatory notes. I needed to learn how to apply the Bible to the world around me and especially to my own situation as a wife and mother. I needed to learn that God could come alive to me through his Word and actually give me messages to act on and promises that I could count on.

Miss Pollock also gave me a small copy of Daily Light, which gives a selection of Bible verses for each day on a related theme.

"This is not instead of your Bible reading," she insisted. "Think of it as iron rations to keep you going until you have time to get to your Bible."

But how was I to find the time to read my Bible? Perhaps that's where being an inveterate reader helped me. I was never without a book or a magazine around, so I decided that I would not allow myself to read anything else until I'd read my Bible verses and the notes for the day. It worked!

Saying prayers at night, usually tucked up in bed, had been a lifelong habit - mostly just a quick recitation of the Lord's prayer followed by any urgent personal requests. I began to extend this so that God could 'bless' my family and a growing list of people. But 'saying prayers' is not quite the same as praying...

All this took a long, long time to develop. Maybe I'm a slow learner too! But gradually I learned that two-way communication with my heavenly Father was possible and that he speaks most often through his own Word. What a wonderful preparation that proved to be when James was pronounced ineducable!

I didn't actually get any special words from the Bible about him, but eventually I did pray, asking God to help us and show us what to do.

And a thought came: Why not seek a second opinion?

Part of the building where David worked in Ballymoney housed a Mother and Baby clinic and David knew the doctor. Might he be willing to see James? He was, and we took him along the following week.

On a small table he had set up various simple tests using brightly coloured blocks and different shapes of wood. James sat on my knee while Doctor Watt gently encouraged him through the tests.

At the end of the session he offered his opinion. "At this stage it is impossible to say what the future holds for James," he said. "He *is* slow, but it all depends on how long he goes on developing."

We left the clinic that blustery afternoon with no false assurances - but at least we had a glimmer of hope!

CHAPTER THREE

The Way Forward

"C for ...?" I asked.

"Cat!" said two-year-old Alison.

"And O is for ...?"

"Orange!" Alison again, a crunchy finger of buttery toast in her hand.

"R is for ...?

"Robin." This time it was James who answered.

"N for ...?

"Noddy!" they chorused, more or less in unison.

It wasn't a formal reading lesson, just the three of us having breakfast together at the kitchen table with a large packet of cornflakes beside us so that we could 'read' the lovely, big letters together.

Learning to read had started with Paul when he was about two years old and mad about books. Even as a one-year-old he would sit contentedly on my knee for as long as half an hour while we turned over the pages of 'My First Book' which we'd borrowed from the Colne Valley library. When we spotted a copy of the same book on our first weekend in Limavady, we bought it and continued to 'read' together.

We made the next step towards reading when he was just over two. I was expecting our second baby that summer, so it was very useful to have a child who enjoyed quiet activities sometimes. His other favourite pastime was going to the garage store and chopping logs for the fire with a small-sized, but real, hatchet. No wonder I encouraged his interest in books!

I had no idea how to teach young children to read. I didn't even know if one should. But I did know that I had a very interested wee boy, so, when he felt like it, I taught him the alphabet the way I'd learned it myself, using phonetic sounds and fitting them to words that he was familiar with. It wasn't long before he was sounding out c-a-t 'cat' and d-o-g 'dog'. In fact, by the time he went to school, the summer he was four, he was already reading most simple words.

Helen hadn't shown quite as much interest as Paul so I hadn't pushed her. But she too had picked up simple phonetic words when she started school, also at four. I never thought of trying with James. He had his own special pace for everything and learning letters would have meant nothing to him when he was just two, though he did like to look at books and he never tore them.

When it came to learning anything I always tried to let each child do the leading. If they showed an interest in anything, I 'followed' by encouraging them. And at that time James was far more interested in feeding the birds that came to the back garden.

At least, in theory! I used to give him scraps of bread or leftover toast to scatter on the grass, which he did all right. But if the birds didn't come quickly enough and I turned my back, I'd find him sitting amongst the scattered crusts, eating them himself!

So it was quite a surprise when Alison reached the two-year-old stage and obviously shared the family fascination for books that James slotted himself into her Corn-Flakes-packet lessons and learnt to recognise most capital letters along with her. He was almost two and a half years older than Alison, but we were really excited to find that he was taking the first step in learning to read.

Just the fact of having Alison growing up alongside him was a wonderful help to James. I'm sure the therapy was two-way because they learned so much together, and became strongly bonded.

"This is how you clean your teeth, James. Watch me!"

Standing on a stool at the bathroom washbasin,

Alison would scrub her teeth vigorously up and down, using lots of squishy pink toothpaste, while James stood, toothbrush in hand, serious eyes intent on the demonstration. Only when she stopped and said "Go on, James. You do it" would he raise the brush to his mouth and make a fair attempt to copy her.

"Look Mummy! James has put on his own sandals!" Hand in hand they came into the kitchen where I was doing the dishes. I'd left them in the other room to finish dressing. James' white strapped sandals were on the wrong feet, but he looked very pleased with himself.

Having Alison around also meant that they could play together while I did necessary housework. Alison usually had the ideas and James co-operated very willingly. Old photographs record the times when they did a clothes swap and James is shown wearing a lovely straw bonnet! Another reminds us of the time they wrapped themselves in fur rugs pretending to be Adam and Eve.

One piece of equipment James loved to play with was my upright German vacuum cleaner. If I left it within reach he would work at it patiently until he had unscrewed every detachable part. We'd noticed that his fingers were slightly spastic, but they were also very strong, and he just loved unscrewing things.

When James was three we had moved house. Rossdowney was getting cramped so when we had the chance to buy a detached house with more bedrooms at a very reasonable price, we jumped at it.

Tyresson was still in Castlerock, though at the opposite end of the village, and it was set in almost an acre of ground. Once we had erected a couple of strategic, slatted wooden fences, the back garden made a large, safe enclosed play area. Sycamores and pine trees lined two sides of this garden and right at the bottom was a very strong, old-fashioned swing.

Alison especially loved this, and not only for swinging. She was a born climber and would shinny up the round steel swing post and 'sit' there for several minutes quite nonchalantly, trousered legs gripping the upright. The sight of her terrified many an adult visitor, but she never fell.

Trees were no problem to her either. Fortunately she was naturally cautious and seemed to know her limits, but she loved to climb up to quite high branches of the sycamores and survey the garden from that vantage point. I think James must have known his limits too, because this was one thing he didn't try to copy. He just didn't have the same co-ordination as Alison and he seemed to accept it. He would chug around quite happily along the pathways on his little red tricycle.

In fact he was an exceptionally even-tempered and happy little boy. Perhaps it was this which made him universally acceptable, even attractive, to people, whether they were acquaintances in the village or complete strangers such as the summer visitors we met on the beach.

I didn't fully appreciate at the time how fortunate we were that James was so readily welcomed wherever he went in our little village community. Later on, when he was older and we holidayed abroad, or even visited relatives in England, we became conscious of turned heads and stares. But not yet. Not in Castlerock. Part of God's mercy in all this was surely the self-confidence he acquired at this early stage in his life.

Whenever it was warm enough I took buckets and spades, towels, a blanket to sit on, books (of course!) and other paraphernalia down to the beach. I usually set up a base beside the dunes and the two - sometimes all four - children would play on the lovely golden sands.

They usually stayed close at hand but occasionally James would stray and most often it was Alison who noticed and went off to retrieve him. He loved to wander from one family group to another. He would smile and squat down beside them and, if they were having a picnic, James generally got a share! He often came back carrying a sausage, or a rather sandy sandwich. Not surprisingly he had no inhibitions about speaking to strangers! In Castlerock, it didn't matter.

Alison didn't have this same sense of freedom. From her very earliest years she seemed to be developing a sense of concern and responsibility for James to a far greater degree than either Paul or Helen. Being older and both at school, they formed a natural unit within the family.

Alison seemed to grow up around James so that, although younger, she soon became the leader. The sense of responsibility and caring for James which started then deepened for as long as we all lived together as a family. Even as a late teenager she would rise from her bed if she had accidentally forgotten to look in and check that he was safely in bed and well tucked up.

When James was almost four, more official carers moved into action. A lady called on us to explain that the first custom-built Special Care Unit in the United Kingdom had been built in the grounds of Coleraine Hospital - just six miles away. They were looking for children like James to be part of the first intake. Would we be interested to let him go there from his fourth birthday?

We certainly were! Until that time we hadn't really given much thought to James' schooling. The shadow of that word 'ineducable' hung over us, though we were determined to teach him as much as we could ourselves. We had never suspected that there was any help like this in the offing. But doesn't the Bible say - Before they call, I will answer?

One sunny October day David and I and the two younger children went along to Coleraine together to see and learn all we could. As we drove into the car park we caught our first glimpse of the low, flat-roofed building set beside the substantial Victorian bulk of the main Hospital.

Alison and James followed us as we were shown round the different halls and classrooms and they were soon eagerly investigating the trays of sand, the gleaming white low-level play sinks and the baskets full of colourful plastic toys. James would have been quite happy for us to leave him there and then!

On that first visit we met some of the boys and girls who would also be joining the Centre. Most were older than James and I found some of them quite distressing to watch. Their uncoordinated movements and strange, inarticulate mouthings made me very uneasy.

I had never been in close contact with pro-foundly handicapped people before and I didn't realise that there were real individuals beneath the sometimes unlovely exteriors. I could only wonder if this was really the right place to send James.

The facilities were obviously first-class and the members of staff that we met seemed to be both caring and competent. But what about the other youngsters with such severe handicaps? Would James be happy amongst them? Would he be helped to realise his full potential?

My doubts deepened when the woman in charge told us that they would not attempt to teach anyone reading or writing skills. I could understand why when I looked at some of the boys and girls, unable to hold up their heads or control the movement of their limbs. But what progress would James be able to make in this environment? Would it be right to let him attend? Yet, equally, would it be right not to?

How good it would have been at that moment to receive a clear directive from the Lord! To hear a voice from heaven saying: This is the next step in my plan for James' life.

But just because we do not receive God's guidance in the way we might like, it does not mean that he is not carefully directing our actions all the same.

David and I returned home and talked it all over. And I talked about it to God too - sometimes in the wee sma' hours when I couldn't sleep.

''Please Father, show us what to do,'' I prayed. ''Prevent us from sending James anywhere that would be wrong for him at this stage.''

Finally we reasoned that, as James would not be accepted at the local Primary School at that time, we might as well let him go to the Coleraine Centre at least for a trial period. After all, it had been built at exactly the right time for our need and in exactly the right place - it was at a mid-way point on David's daily route to work.

So on the 21st November 1963, his fourth birthday, James enrolled in Coleraine Special Care Centre. David had agreed to pick up two other local boys and deliver them with James to the Centre each morning. In return for this service the local authority paid for a taxi to bring them all home at 3.30 in the afternoon.

For the next twelve months we re-arranged our daily living to fit in with James' new pattern. He settled into the routine beautifully, happy to go off with his Daddy in the morning and glad to see us when he came back in the afternoon.

Although I hardly liked to admit it even to myself, I appreciated the release from the constant watchfulness I'd needed with James around. And I enjoyed having my two-year-old Alison on her own for several hours each day.

As the weeks went by I watched for progress in James but I didn't really notice any. He was very much just himself, speaking very clearly now in a rather high-pitched treble and even singing some nursery rhymes with us.

One of his favourites was Hickory, Dickory Dock. I think he liked that one because it reminded him of the two white mice we had at that time. James loved to play with them and to try to pick them up in his fat wee fingers. I squirmed when I saw him putting a tiny, pink-footed creature down the neck of his pullover, but he just squealed in delight. He had absolutely no fear of them - or of any other animals.

That was one more thing I had to watch when we were out. When we walked around the village James had a passion for closing garden gates. None were allowed to be left ajar when he was on patrol. And it was as he went about these gatekeeping duties that he encountered various cats and dogs. His instinct was always to squat down - or reach up - and stroke them. Usually his attentions were either accepted or ignored. But I always felt I needed to be on hand for the occasional bark or sharp swipe of a cat's claw. So far we had avoided any serious harm and James still loved animals - and rhymes about them.

But it was at *home* that he'd learned the rhymes. I found it hard to know if he was learning *anything* at the Centre. I did notice one change that I was not too happy about. He began to make peculiar noises to himself. Sounds which were not like James at all.

Unintelligible grunting sounds which reminded me of some of the boys I'd seen at the Centre. He had been there for almost a year when I became aware of this and again the old uneasiness began to stir in me. When his fifth birthday approached, I asked David: "Don't you think we should see if James could move to some other place? I'm sure he could learn more than he'll ever be taught at the Centre."

The trouble was that, as far as we knew, there wasn't any other educational Centre locally which would be able to help James. Yet it seemed a shame that he shouldn't have every chance to learn all he could. I recalled Dr. Watt's words: It all depends on how long he goes on developing.

So again I prayed that God would show us the next move. I prayed without realising how many threads would be involved in his answer - far more than we were aware of at the time. The threads of my husband's work and the place we lived would play a significant part.

~~~~~~

"As a little boy James seemed to sense that he mattered a whole lot. One hadn't far to look before guessing why. He mattered at home and had his full quota of love from the whole family." Betty Pollock (Neighbour), Castlerock, 1991

~~~~~~

CHAPTER FOUR

Learning To Trust

"I heard some interesting news today."

David's homecoming remarks tantalised me as I peeled potatoes for our evening meal and handed the pieces to James to plop into the saucepan of water.

"What about?"

"They're creating a school dental job in a new area. Based on Limavady. I might apply for it."

That was plenty for my mind to work on as David carried James away into the living room to play with the others while I got on with the meal preparations in peace.

My first thought was that Limavady was in the wrong direction - for James anyway. Coleraine and the Centre were east; Limavady was 17 miles to the south west.

For one moment I wondered if I might be able to take him to the Centre by public transport, but I quickly realised it would be impossible. Might the authorities be willing to grant the boys a taxi each way? Always supposing David got the new job, of course.

He applied and went for an interview in Limavady. This small market town where we'd spent our first weekend in Ireland served a well-populated farming area. The town centre has one wide street and several smaller ones packed with amazing quantities of chemist's shops, draper's and public houses. It is only a few miles from the sea and overlooked by the green slopes of Benevenagh mountain.

At the interview David discovered another very interesting piece of information. Limavady actually had a special school for Educationally Sub-Normal boys - Greystone Hall. It was the next grade up from Special Care and James just *might* fit in there. It was an exciting thought for James' future. But it depended on so many things and the first essential was for David to get the job.

He did! And almost at once he made an appointment to see Mr. Carrington, Headmaster of Greystone Hall. The school was set in attractive wooded grounds on the outskirts of the town. At that time most of the pupils were admitted as boarders from seven years of age. But there were also a few classes for younger day pupils so, as James would soon have his sixth birthday, Mr. Carrington was willing to accept him - *if* the psychologist considered James mentally able, and *if* we could arrange daily transport to and from the school.

Entirely due to David's new job coming at this precise moment, transport was, once again, no problem. David worked more or less school hours and his base was only a few streets away from the school.

Mr. Carrington suggested that James attend for a trial week so that he could observe him for himself before calling in the psychologist.

The Special Care people in Coleraine were not enthusiastic when we explained what we were doing.

"What's the point? they said. "He'll never learn anything and you'll only unsettle him. And he'll have to come back here in the end."

I tried to put their words out of my mind and prayed that God would help our little boy in this new situation. I felt sure it must be the Lord who was orchestrating all these fine details.

By the end of the first week Mr. Carrington had made his own, well-qualified assessment.

"This is exactly the right place for James," he said. "Leave him with us on a daily basis. I'll take care of the formalities."

And so James began his career at Greystone Hall. David ferried him back and forth daily and

James began to *learn*! All sorts of things! He had a pack of five small dark red cards in an envelope with words which he had to recognise. 'Car ... coat ... cup ... tree ... book'. We went through these faithfully each evening for his 'homework'. And gradually the pack grew and the contents changed. The method was different to my earlier one but James was actually managing to read!

When he tried to write he confirmed what we had long suspected. He was left-handed and his hand movement was not very good.

One thing which delighted us was that he was obviously being given teaching with a really Christian emphasis. Naturally James couldn't explain this to us - in fact we only discovered it by accident when the family was driving home from town one Saturday.

David had to brake suddenly as a car came out of a side road without warning. The sudden stop was a shock for us all.

"My! That was nearly the end of us!" David said.

"And we'd all have gone to heaven," Helen piped up from the back.

"I don't want to go to heaven today!" David smiled as we slowly gathered speed again. Then James leaned forward and put his hand on David's shoulder.

"Not everybody can go to heaven, Dad," he said seriously. "You have to ask Jesus to wash you clean and come into your heart."

I held my breath, knowing that David was at a kind of crisis point in his faith. He had, in fact, stopped going to church or Sunday School until he could get things sorted out. He was determined above all not to be a hypocrite.

So how had James grasped this basic gospel truth so surely - clearly enough to be able to apply it so accurately to the situation? I knew I'd never been so specific with James at home. I wouldn't have thought he could have grasped such ideas. Gentle questions later revealed that his class teacher, Miss Nutt (Bounty Bar to most of the boys!) had told them that everybody needed to ask Jesus into their heart and then, when they died, they would go to heaven.

For the next few months family life flowed on uneventfully. Paul had finished primary school and moved to Coleraine Academy travelling there each day by bus. Helen was at the Hezlett Primary School, a mile inland from Castlerock where she had been joined by a rather reluctant four-year-old Alison.

In the country as a whole more overt stirrings of political unrest were beginning to be heard - at least by those who had ears to hear such things. Being a mother-of-four, and an English outsider at that, these stirrings did not manage to disturb my daily life. There had been sandbags round the entrance to the village police station when we arrived in '56 and we'd long grown used to the sight of armed pairs of 'B' Specials walking along the railway line at the foot of the garden on their way to guard the nearby tunnels on the Belfast-Londonderry line. But as far as we could see, nothing 'political' happened in Castlerock.

We'd learned to take for granted the Catholic/Protestant divide which not only channelled us to our different places of worship each Sunday, but which also segregated the children into rigorously separate schools. We realised that we'd never be 'natives' - though the children developed two distinct accents - Yorkshire at home and Ulster with their pals. Yet, in spite of all this, Castlerock really felt like home to us. There had been, however, one slight but significant shaking of the roots.

A colleague had arrived unexpectedly from Yorkshire one day and invited David out for the evening. I never usually prayed about my husband's evenings out, but this time I felt that I should definitely commit their conversation to the Lord and ask him to control it - though I had no idea what it would be about.

The memory of that evening is crystal clear.

When David returned alone at midnight, I was sitting on the swing at the bottom of the garden, praying. Once I knew the children were sound asleep I liked to go and pray outside in that quiet place under the trees. David guessed where I was and came down the garden to find me.

"Did you have a good evening?" I asked.

"Mmm. Different," he said. "Neil has some interesting plans."

"They don't affect us, do they?"

"They might. Come on - let's check if the kids are OK and go and walk on the beach for a while."

I felt apprehensive even then.

As we walked along the hard, flat sand with the sea whispering silver in the moonlight, David told me about Neil's plans to expand his dental practice in Yorkshire. He wanted to set up a surgery in another town and to do that he would need someone to work part of the time in his Huddersfield practice. He'd come to ask if David would be interested.

"And are you?" I felt cold all over. Frozen by the thought of moving back to Huddersfield.

"It'd only be for a few years, four at the most. And it'd be well paid."

I said nothing. We walked beside the splashing waves in silence. A most uncharacteristic silence. Normally I'd have been talking fifteen to the dozen, working out my ideas and reactions as I spoke. But

I hadn't the slightest desire to speak. I felt numb inside. My brain was thinking back to my one-off prayer earlier in the evening when I'd committed their conversation to God. I certainly hadn't expected this!

But then, neither could I doubt that the God who had prompted the prayer was also in the answer. What I wanted to reply was: NO! NO! NO! I don't want to go back to Huddersfield, even for a short time. I don't want to leave Castlerock - ever!

I also knew quite clearly that that answer was *my* will. But maybe it wasn't *God's* will for me - for us. Yet what if it was where God was wanting us to go ... how could I say 'No' to him?

Still without speaking we turned back on our tracks. We couldn't leave the children unattended for more than a very short time.

"Come on," David said gently. "Say something. Tell me what you think."

"I think ... you should do whatever seems right to you."

I couldn't say any more. Inwardly I was committing the whole situation to the Lord. I didn't know what he'd have in mind. Maybe we would have to leave Castlerock and go back to Huddersfield. If that was what he wanted, then I'd have to ask him to help me become willing to go. I knew I wasn't at that stage yet. But because of that unusual but surely prompted earlier prayer, I knew I had to leave the outcome in his hands and accept whatever he sent.

I did wish we could have prayed about it together but we had not done that for quite some time. In fact I wasn't sure where David was spiritually.

The prospect of moving filled my mind in the days that followed. Yet I still didn't want to talk about it to David very much. I felt constrained to keep quiet and let God do all the mind-moving. He is so capable of it. And I can be too manipulative!

In reality God was manipulating *me*. He did not, in fact, require us to return to Yorkshire after all. Nothing came of Neil's proposals and we had no offer to accept or refuse. But the roots which had buried themselves so deeply in Castlerock's sandy soil had been shaken so that, when another job change possibility appeared on the horizon, my reaction to the thought of uprooting our family from Castlerock was quite mild. How graciously the Lord prepares our way! How well he knows our human frailty.

This time the job was in private practice and thirty miles due south of Castlerock in the town of Magherafelt. Yet again, the dilemma of James' schooling came to the fore. Without David's daily transport to and from school, Greystone Hall would be out of the question.

Unless James could become a boarder ... The minimum age for boarders was seven - but James had had his seventh birthday a few months earlier. David decided to discuss the situation with Mr. Carrington.

We hadn't expected a negative answer, and indeed Mr. Carrington was loath to give it.

"I'm sorry," he said, "but there are no free places for boarders. We have one boy leaving at Easter but we also have a waiting list and the place has already been promised to the first boy on the list."

So what were we to do about James? At all costs we wanted to avoid having to send him back to the Special Care Centre in Coleraine because we wanted his education to continue. Perhaps the local primary school could help? We found that legally they couldn't refuse to take James, but the Headmaster, though sympathetic, was not enthusiastic.

"Our classes are so big ... all over thirty. It would be impossible for the teacher to give James the attention he needs and he'd end up just sitting there. I don't think it would be good for him."

So we moved into the Easter holiday period with no solution in sight. Except that I might have to try to teach him myself at home. I didn't feel equipped for that at all.

"Trust in the Lord with all your heart and lean

not on your own understanding.'' The words came in one of my daily readings.

"To trust," I told myself, "is not to go over a situation in your head day and night. To trust is to have confidence that the Lord has a plan - a *good* plan - in mind. And he is more than capable of making it happen."

Two days before the schools re-started the phone rang. "Mrs. McKay? This is Mr. Carrington," said the cheerful voice. "I can offer you a place for James to come to Greystone Hall as a boarder immediately after the holiday. Can you have him ready?''

I nearly dropped the phone from sheer relief as he went on to explain that the first boy's parents had turned down the vacant place and, as he thought it important that James should not have a break in his education, he was waiving the rest of the list and offering the vacancy to James! Praise the Lord!

~~~~~~~~~~~~~~~~~~~~~~~~~~~~~~~~~~~~~~~

"I remember that James was soft and sensitive - we only had to say 'Poor James' in a sad tone of voice, and he'd cry." Helen, Israel, 1991

~~~~~~~~~~~~~~~~~~~~~~~~~~~~~~~~~~~~~~~

CHAPTER FIVE

Fruits Of Continuance

In the late spring of 1967, with James happily ensconced as a boarder at Greystone Hall, and David not-so-happily driving over thirty miles of winding country roads to Magherafelt and back each day, the question of leaving Castlerock came up again.

I sensed no loud inward protests this time. More a feeling that the end of a stage might have come. It might be God's time for us to move. Consciously and confidently I handed the whole situation over to him. When we learn to do this - and *remember* to do it - the peace of mind which comes is as wonderful as he promised.

We put our lovely seaside home on the market and waited ... and waited. People came to view it, made approving noises, but no firm offers.

The early summer passed. Pink and white roses rioted over the rustic wooden pergolas and bunches of succulent blackcurrants clustered in profusion on the bushes. But no one was tempted to buy.

Perhaps God wanted us to stay on in Castlerock after all? Suitable houses seemed to be scarce in Magherafelt too.

But one day David had news. He had actually been to see a house, but he refused to describe it to me.

"I'll take you to see it on Friday," he promised. "It's different and if you don't like it, just say so. There'll be plenty more. It's up to you."

I hate having an onus thrust on to me like that. But I have learnt that I can always pass the buck one stage further - on to God! He *really* knows!

So the night before, and as we walked up the driveway towards the house on the Friday morning, I prayed in my heart, "Lord, show me if this is where you want us. Make it clear to me if this is the house we should buy." I couldn't imagine how he would but...

It certainly looked attractive - if you like modern houses - set in its own sloping, well kept, tree-lined grounds. Timber clad, the huge window and balcony gave the upstairs lounge an outdoor, almost 'woodsy' feel, while the open-plan interior certainly fitted David's description of 'different'.

As we moved about the four living levels, I tried to imagine how our family would use the rooms. Most were obvious - kitchen, dining room, two lounges - one in front and one which had been added on at the back. The top section of bathroom and three bedrooms would easily accommodate the children and a fourth room at ground level could also be used as a bedroom. It was so totally different in character from Tyresson, yet attractive in its own way.

I was conscious that David was keeping quiet, leaving me to form my own impressions while the owner led us from room to room.

"My husband used this room as a study," she said, showing us into another ground floor room, lined on one side with bookshelves and cupboards.

"This could be yours," David smiled. "You'd soon fill it with books."

I liked the feel of the room. I liked the light oak woodwork and the square window which gave on to the neighbours' gardens and trees. I could imagine myself here.

It was then that I turned and saw the picture - the only one I had noticed in the house. It was just a simple print of mountains and a stream, but it had some words printed along the base. At the time I didn't realise they were from the tenth chapter of Hebrews. The words stood out for me, communicating vibrantly: 'a new, living way which he opened for us'.

It would be exactly that - a new way of living - if we moved from the seaside to the country; from a traditional house to this modern one; from a place where we were known, to a town where we knew no-one.

In my heart I knew quite surely at that moment that God was quietly giving me his answer from his own Word via that picture on the wall.

We bought the house that August and named it 'Lisbrega'- the house on the hill. We were quite unaware how many other people had also been keen to buy it. We later learned from the Lynns, a local couple who had also tried to buy the house (they became and still are our very good friends), that when they failed to get the house, they had to rent a council house and buy building land, so scarce was property at that time. God had truly opened a way for us.

We moved in time for Paul, Helen and Alison all to start the autumn term at the Rainey Endowed School a hundred yards down the road. It was a school where children were placed according to their ability. Paul went into the second year of the senior school, Helen into Primary six and Alison, aged five and wearing a diminutive, black pleated gymslip and white blouse, slotted into Primary Three.

Greystone Hall was now thirty miles away in a north-westerly direction, but once he was settled back there, our move did not seem to affect James at all. Every week we received a painstakingly penned letter from him. It was obviously copied and hardly varied from one week to another.

"Dear Mum and Dad, Thank you for your letter. I hope you are well. I am learning to tie my shoelaces. Love, James. X X X"

How precious those letters were from a son who had managed to learn to write, in spite of the experts' gloomy predictions!

Not that James was always a model pupil. With his pals Alec and Ian he sometimes got into trouble. Once they strayed out of bounds into a farmer's field and suffered the consequences of a visit to Mr. Carrington's office and some sharp words which he has never forgotten.

It was Alec and Ian also who inadvertently intensified one of James' problems.

They all shared the same dormitory which, after the pillow fights had subsided, was left in darkness apart from a corridor light which glowed dimly through a glass porthole window in the door. Alec and Ian somehow managed to convince James that there were ghosts on the fire escape just outside and that the devil himself was 'under the floor' and if he ever dared to get out of bed for any reason - even for the toilet - the devil would get him. "The devil comes into the toilet," they warned. "You can hear him."

All this was quite enough to keep James firmly anchored in bed. He would rather face the consequences of a wet bed than the unknown threat of being caught by the devil.

It didn't happen every night, but often enough for me to become annoyed when it was reported to me. Because James never wet the bed at home, even during the whole time of the long summer holidays. Nothing I said, and nothing the staff said once I'd explained to them, could remove the fears the boys had planted in his mind. He remained vulnerable during the whole of his stay at Greystone Hall.

Toilet training was one area where we had had problems earlier. In particular James would delay emptying his bowels until the last possible moment. As no amount of coaxing produced the desired result, I had to watch until I saw the telltale, stiff-legged walk and then hustle him to the toilet where I exhorted him to 'Push! Push!' For years it was the only way to get results.

I explained to the staff at Greystone Hall, but obviously they couldn't give each boy such individual surveillance, so that problem too remained with James for the duration of his stay there.

Once a month we were allowed to have James home for the weekend. He would be waiting for Alison and me when we arrived after school, no longer dressed in the smart, grey uniform provided by the school, but in his own clothes.

"You've got new shoes," he said once as he scrambled into the car where I was still sitting at the wheel. No changes, however small, escaped his observant eyes, though his manner of observing sometimes caused embarrassment to us, if not to him. He had a habit of gazing at people intently, and usually open-mouthed.

"Don't gawp, James!" his sisters would tartly remind him until we evolved a code word 'Boca' - Spanish for mouth - which did the trick without being so obvious to other people.

These close observations enabled him to mimic other people very well.

"Shall I show you how Mr. Hall drinks?" he would offer. And then he would mime someone draining a glass, ending by opening and closing his lips rapidly and repeatedly.

Once when we were on holiday visiting friends in France, they took us on a tour of a chateau. The touring group was typically cosmopolitan. Just as typically, James left us and wormed his way to the front, but instead of paying attention to the official guide - who was speaking French in any case - he gazed up at the red-swathed head of a Sikh gentleman. Having gazed his fill he turned to us and said in his clearest Irish voice, "He must have been in a wild bad crash, Dad!'' We just hoped the man was not an English speaker!

Language didn't seem to be any barrier to James because, only a few minutes later, he was wearing the guide's gold-braided navy cap and carrying his torch!

What a difference James made when he was with us, even for just a weekend. The house seemed suddenly to come alive as he and Alison chased each other or played together, often shrieking with laughter. They also loved to have a more-than-willing Helen read to them, story after story, often cuddled up three in a bed. His occasional presence showed us how quiet life was without him; how incomplete we were as a family when he was not there. When we took him back to school on Sunday evenings, we all missed him.

Did James miss us? He didn't seem to. He certainly never made any fuss about going back. Once, when I asked him if he'd rather be a boarder or live at home as he used to, he answered quite positively: ''I'd rather be a boarder 'cos you get pocket money.''

Through his presence in Limavady James also built up another very special relationship. One of David's former colleagues from RAF days lived very near to Greystone Hall. 'Uncle' Sam and his wife, Mary, often took James out on Saturdays and

Sundays when he fitted in with David and Susan, their own young children.

James got so used to being with them that, if we were also invited over for tea, it was to Uncle Sam rather than to us that James turned when he needed anything. By this time, however, James was fairly self-sufficient. He could tie his laces and even knot his tie. Sam and Mary were all part of God's loving provision for James at that time.

Scholastically James was better at reading and writing than at sums, especially when more than ten fingers were involved. In fact, we had one unusual demonstration of his reading ability when we were on holiday in Donegal.

We had rented a caravan for two weeks on a site at Marble Hill. We drove to Londonderry, then across the border and on to the rough Donegal roads which seem to specialise in twists, turns and pot-holes, via Letterkenny to Marble Hill. It was a dull and distinctly chilly July day and not long after we arrived, the rain started. No ordinary rain either, but the stair-rod, caravan-roof-drumming variety which actually washed out some of the road bridges we had crossed earlier in the day. We couldn't have taken the same route home had we wanted to!

Later that evening, in that incredible weather, there was a knock on the door of our caravan. We opened it to find totally unexpected friends from

Yorkshire, dripping wet! We hadn't seen Robert and Corinne for years but they were touring Ireland and, having failed to find us at home, they had been redirected by neighbours to this remote corner of Donegal.

We spent a great evening, squashed together in the rather small sitting section of the caravan, with the steady drumbeat of relentless Donegal rain as a background to our conversation.

"And how's Jamie then?" Robert said at one point. We never called him anything but James, but other people sometimes rearranged his name.

"He's doing fine. He's at school and he can even read now," I told him.

"I don't believe it. Is it true, Jamie? Can you read?"

"Yes," James himself answered.

"Show me. Where's your book?" Robert demanded a demonstration. James produced a simple Ladybird reader and Robert tucked him in on the seat beside him and took the book, flicking through the pages.

"There," he said at last, "let's see if you can read that page." And he handed the book to James, deliberately upside down.

James accepted the book, continued to hold it upside down, and proceeded to read every word on the page correctly! In his own quiet way, James provided a most effective proof for Robert. We were just as amazed as Robert was, but James can still read print upside down with ease.

It was on that same Donegal holiday, which continued wet and blustery, that the children and I passed some time memorising part of the thirteenth chapter of First Corinthians. I chose a modern version so that they would understand it and received a lovely confirmation when David allowed me to slip away and attend a short service in the church at nearby Dunfanaghy. Starting at verse four the minister read and preached on the very verses we had been learning!

"Love is patient, love is kind ..." There's nothing like two wet weeks in a caravan with four children to learn *that* lesson!

Perhaps it is only as we look back from time to time that we see how God allows phases of quiet continuance to alternate with periods of change in our lives. What happens in those periods of continuance is less dramatic but perhaps equally important as the more eventful times. Moreover, as mother of a family, I was increasingly, if with regrettable slowness, becoming aware of how much my life, and particularly the state of my relationship with Jesus, affected every family member.

I had continued to read my Bible and notes every day, eventually moving from Daily Bread to Daily

Notes. Slowly, slowly I was gaining an overall picture of the Bible and becoming familiar with it. I remember how delighted I was when I completed my first full reading of it!

I didn't always find it easy to understand, even with notes, but at first I still had access to our friend Willie. In fact, when we moved to Tyresson, his potato field bordered with our garden and many a time when I saw him working there, I went out and joined him in the field and plied him with my awkward questions.

On other days Willie would pay me a visit in the afternoon and he would insist that I carry on with my ironing while I told him some of the amazing new truths I was discovering, or how God had been speaking to me as I read.

The timing of my Bible reading had changed too with the changing pattern of family life. In Tyresson I read late at night when everybody, including David, was fast asleep in bed. I enjoyed the quietness, the freedom from interruptions and the open-endedness of those hours. I often rounded off my reading session by praying kneeling at a low window in one of the children's bedrooms. From there I could look out over the whole village and pray round it before remembering my family and missionary friends in different parts of the world.

Many of the missionaries Miss Pollock had

introduced to me had become my own friends as we exchanged letters. Most, but not all, have now retired from working abroad, but we still keep in touch by letter. Indeed most, but not all, I have met in person. All have added interest and encouragement to my life and to the children's.

Perhaps it was their influence as well as my Bible reading which affected the content of my general reading too.

I had regularly subscribed to a monthly women's magazine, but one day I found that these magazines were sitting in a pile unread for lack of time. So I cancelled my order. ''I'll read through what Christian books there are,'' I told myself, estimating that it would take me about six months, ''and then I'll renew my order.'' To date I have not re-ordered the magazine and I'm still reading Christian books non-stop! What a lot I have owed to them from the very start!

Life with four young children in those days didn't leave much time for friendships, and in Castlerock there were not many people of my age to be friends with. And, because I was always happy with a book I found I could choose my teacher and advance at my own rate. As the years passed I savoured the teachings of Oswald Chambers, Isobel Kuhn, Watchman Nee and Amy Carmichael as well as the simpler, yet profound thoughts of Corrie ten Boom. Later E M Blaiklock, C S Lewis and John Stott, amongst others, became my tutors.

Once the children were a little bit older I was free to find friends from a little further afield. One of these lived in Coleraine and I shall always be grateful to Frankie Crawford for introducing me to the delights of women's Bible studies.

I went to the first one with some trepidation. I had no idea what was going to happen and I was not eager to have my scriptural ignorance exposed in public. The women in that first group were warm, friendly and very welcoming. But I was also aware that they were for the most part the wives of ministers, doctors, teachers and even a doctor of theology! I determined to keep my mouth shut.

I need not have worried. First and foremost they were women ... women with faults and failings, with personal heartaches and needs ... women who were keen to meet together to find Christ's help in his Word. The thread of Bible study with groups of women started then when I was still living in Castlerock and, by God's grace, it has continued without a break to this day of writing.

Writing - that was another part of my life that God touched. The fact that my two short stories had been published earlier seemed to prove that I had some kind of aptitude for writing. But I found

I had lost all desire to write romantic fiction. It seemed so pointless.

"But if you can use my writing skills in other ways," I told the Lord, "please show me."

He did. In one of the magazines Mary Pollock gave me there was an appeal for writers of children's short stories for Scripture Union's 'Adventurer' leaflets. I enquired and was asked to submit a children's story, with a suitable teaching point. After that a pencil and notebook accompanied our sorties to the beach and, after trying it out on my own captive audience, I sent off my first children's story.

Ten days later I got a letter of acceptance, providing I would allow one or two alterations. I even received payment of one guinea - one pound and five pence!

That was when I made an almost Jacob-like bargain with God.

"If you will give me time and ideas to write about, and the ability to write them acceptably, I'll offer my writing to you and you can have the money too."

Without realising it, I had entered upon a long period of continuance of writing a variety of stories for Scripture Union.

The very practical question of how God wanted me to use the money was one of the things he used to teach me to make a small venture of faith and to learn to hear his voice directing me from his Word.

It was through reading a missionary magazine that I was first confronted with the idea of sponsoring a boy in a Christian orphanage in Korea.

"Lord, if you really want me to do this," I asked him, "will you give me enough acceptances to cover the cost of his upkeep?"

Before making the commitment I also cleared it with David that he would make good any shortfall. How faithless can you get?

So I embarked on the project and we adopted Won Jong Yul. Quite apart from the writing angle, I hoped it would make Christian concern for others in need more real to the children. We exchanged photographs and sent the occasional letter and birthday gift and we prayed for him together.

I sent off the agreed monthly donation of £3.50 and at the same time I continued to write for Scripture Union. There was a limit to the number of stories they could use and I didn't try to keep balanced books, though I faithfully recorded each cheque I received in a little red Cash Book. I also felt I should include a tithe of what little money came to me personally in birthday gifts.

The exciting moment came at the end of the first year when I added up my writing income from August 1962 to July 1963 and compared it with the steady monthly outgoing payments for the same period. They tallied exactly! God *had* provided all I asked including the money for Won Jong Yul, and I hadn't needed to ask for any subsidy!

The next question was, would he do it again? Should I make the same commitment for another year? In one way I didn't feel we could abandon the boy - yet I also felt I must check with our heavenly Father. And that was when he really took my breath away!

I had been praying about it of course, but the day was fast approaching when my next payment - or a terminating letter - was due.

David also knew I was praying so, when I got God's answer from his Word in one of my daily Bible readings the day before the next cheque was due to be sent off, I couldn't wait to share it with him.

"You know I was asking God what he wanted me to do about Won Jong Yul?" I said when he came home from work. "Well, listen to what I read today."

I picked up my J B Phillips New Testament and read aloud from it. "Here is my opinion in the matter. I think it would be a good thing for you, who were the first a year ago to think of helping, as well as the first to give, to carry through what you then intended to do. Finish it, then, as well as you can, and show that you can complete what you set out to do with as much efficiency as you showed readiness to begin. After all, the important thing is to be willing to give as much as we can - that is what God accepts, and no one is asked to give what he has not got.''

I paused for breath as David said: "That can't be in the Bible.''

"But it is!'' I insisted, holding the book out for him so that he could read for himself. "It's in the eighth chapter of Paul's second letter to the Corinthians.''

How could I disobey such a wonderfully clear word? I was so grateful for it and amazed at the same time that God should speak so clearly - to *me*! I could easily understand how he could give messages to missionaries or other special people, but to *me*? That was just fantastic! I treasured the thought - and kept on writing.

I had a moment of trepidation shortly afterwards when the contributions had to be increased, but I decided that God could probably manage to supply another 75p a month, as of course he did. He enabled me to support Won Jong Yul until 1974 when they wrote to say he had left the Home and sadly, we have had no more news of him. But we continue to entrust him to our Father.

One feature of the relatively peaceful periods of

our lives is that we never know how long they are going to last, though we rarely anticipate their ending.

But we cannot prevent change and in the late 1960's change and general unrest in Northern Ireland were becoming impossible to ignore, even for outsiders like us. Living in Magherafelt seemed to sharpen the issues.

We had friends in both the Protestant and Roman Catholic communities. Indeed David's employer was Roman Catholic, and they got on well. But it became increasingly difficult to avoid issues, when Scottish soldiers were shot. "They shouldn't be here," was David's employer's attitude.

David still hadn't resumed church attendance when we moved to Magherafelt but I became part of a real family church in the country hamlet of Lecumpher, three miles away from our house. I first went there because it was part of a linked charge and I could attend church at the same time as the children were at Sunday School in the sister church in town. That left us free to visit James in the afternoon.

I also helped start a Christian Endeavour group with the teenagers of the two churches and this provided me with many learning opportunities. Just how do you present Jesus' teaching to love your enemies when those enemies might well be setting fire to your father's barn while you're at the meeting? It actually happened. Yet I was not at liberty to alter Christ's words.

Little by little life became less pleasant. Walking home from a CE meeting one night, I went to post a birthday card at the Post Office, only to find a bayonet across the mouth of the box.

"What's inside?" a soldier asked.

"Only a birthday card."

"OK, go ahead," he said, removing the bayonet for a moment.

Magherafelt was a market town thirty miles from just about everywhere it seemed - Limavady, Castlerock, Londonderry and Belfast anyway. It was larger than Castlerock and more divided politically. When we moved there it had quite a nice shopping centre. But then the bombings started and one by one the best shops were burned out. It was not pleasant to be in town, with or without children, when the sirens went and fire engines were speeding about.

In an attempt to prevent these fire-bombings, Magherafelt and many other towns eventually had all their roads blocked. A single, armed and guarded entry point gave car access, after scrutiny, to the town by day. At night no-one was allowed to enter or leave by car. This meant long, time-wasting detours and much inconvenience but it was a necessary precaution and even then some bombers managed to slip through with their easily concealed, deadly packages.

We got used to having our bags and sometimes our bodies searched as we went in and out of some shops, but it was not pleasant. We stopped going to Belfast. Car parks were surrounded by barbed wire and guarded, while armed soldiers peered down from the rooftops of high buildings nearby. More than one of our friends had to abandon their car in a multi-storeypark in Belfast when there was a bomb scare in the building.

As 1971 progressed we began to ask ourselves: were we crazy to go on living there?

CHAPTER SIX

Go Forward With Confidence

"Three soldiers were killed today when the vehicle they were travelling in was blown up near Enniskillen. In the Bogside district of Londonderry, rioting again broke out and soldiers fired rubber bullets into crowds of stone-throwing youths."

David and I were lying in bed listening, as we always did, to the midnight news bulletin. We didn't want to. It was always a catalogue of bad news. And yet, somehow we couldn't resist switching on each news time. We felt we had to know what was happening.

It was no way to prepare ourselves for a good night's sleep. But, like thousands of others, we nightly covered ourselves with this grey blanket of depressing news.

At eight o'clock next morning we switched on again. The sun was shining - through the window the day looked good. Surely the news would be too?

"Forty buses were burnt out in Belfast last night when a bomb exploded..."

Explosions ... burnings ... pub bombings ... ambushes ... rioting ... nothing changed. Only the details varied from day to day, from town to town.

We had been to Scotland in February that year, 1971, for a short, early holiday, staying as usual with Granny in Forfar. It had been good to get away for a while from 'the situation'. But once we were back, we found ourselves fitting back into our routine of schools and work, trying to ignore the inconveniences of road blocks and the probability of being stopped and searched if we had to drive at night for any reason.

We had a summer holiday in Forfar that year too, again invading our long-suffering Granny's bungalow. James had especially enjoyed sleeping up in her capacious and comfortable attic with the others. He was eleven and 'a big boy' now - at least he had lost all his childhood chubbiness and his long, thin legs and knobbly knees looked best in long trousers.

As he grew taller it became more apparent that it was physically impossible for him to stand straight-legged for more than just a few seconds. His knees had to be slightly bent in order to keep his balance. His feet were rather mis-shapen, and his toes especially became very twisted, though he could walk quite long distances with ease, as he proved when we picnicked that summer in the Angus glens.

The doctors and chiropodists we consulted said nothing could be done and it didn't matter as long as he could walk, so things were best left alone. We took their advice, provisionally.

In August my own mother came for her annual holiday and even then we had never seriously got to grips with the possibility of actually uprooting ourselves and leaving Northern Ireland.

But when she had gone home the question 'To stay or not to stay?' began to infiltrate our conversation more and more.

The final news bulletin each night would make us decide to sell up and go.   Early morning optimism in the moments before the news next day would make us ask ourselves if we were just panicking about something that would be over in a month or two.   After all, the whole population couldn't up and leave - surely something would be sorted out soon?

But by evening the repeated news bulletins would have eroded our optimism. What should we do?

We felt unsettled - as if we were living in a grey fog. We couldn't see the way forward for ourselves or for our children. Especially for our children. In a few years Paul could be at University which could mean living in Belfast. Not an attractive prospect, if things went on as they were.

Other people, especially farmers with land and people with businesses - all with relatives - might not be able to leave easily, but we only had a house and job to hold us and both, we hoped, would be replaceable.

On the other hand, for fifteen years life had been good here and we had made many friends. We wanted to be very sure before we gave it all up.

"What do you really think we should do?" David asked one evening when the children were in bed.

How weary I was of asking myself that question! This time my answer seemed to speak itself, the words surprising me even as I spoke them. But isn't this how God sometimes implants his guidance?

"I think we should ask somebody who is right outside our situation," I said. If we were to explain the way we were feeling to someone else, it might help to clarify our thoughts. And they might be able to give us more balanced advice.

"Let's ask Willie," David replied without hesitation. I was a bit surprised, but very pleased, by his choice. Surprised, because we had rarely seen Willie since we moved to Magherafelt. And when we did meet, he was always disappointed that

David seemed to have turned away from his earlier love for Jesus.

The following day, Wednesday, was a free day for David so he rang to see if Willie would be available for us to visit him. He didn't explain the reason for the visit and Willie must have been surprised at such a request coming out of the blue, but he willingly agreed to see us next morning.

It is at times like this that it is particularly strengthening to know that one has access to God through prayer. Not only did I pray myself as we drove the thirty miles to Castlerock on that sunny September morning, but I also knew that Willie would be praying and entrusting the encounter to the Lord. I asked that God would guide the conversation and give Willie wisdom to know what to say. Above all, I wanted God to indicate *his* way forward through Willie's words.

Willie welcomed us both warmly, but shortly afterwards I went for a walk, leaving the men together for their talk. This is the way things were done in Northern Ireland. Women were expected to keep very much in the background.

Even when I rejoined them over an hour later, nothing was said about their discussion so I had to wait until we were driving home for lunch to get the verdict.

"Willie thinks we should leave Northern Ireland,'' he said. ''From a personal point of view he doesn't want us to go, but he thinks it would be best for all our family if we did. He can't see that anything will be resolved here for a long time to come.''

I realised as we drove that I was not really surprised. A little bit sad perhaps, and yet, deep down, I knew that God had spoken through Willie. I felt the fog had lifted a little and we could begin to move forward, mentally at least. So where did we go from here?

Neither of us wanted to go back to Yorkshire. And we knew from the Dental Journal that jobs were available all over Britain - in Thurso and Truro and all points in between!

We discussed the pros and cons of many areas and it was when we began to cast around for an actual destination that I noticed what was written on the fly-leaf of my Daily Light. 'Aberdeen 1969'. I had treated myself to a new copy in an Aberdeen bookshop while on holiday. It might be quite a nice place to live, I thought, and it would have good schools and a University for the children. Maybe even something for James?

I didn't say anything to David. It would be interesting to hear his ideas, uninfluenced by mine.

One day he arrived home with a copy of the Dental Journal. ''There's a job here I might apply for,'' he said, handing me the magazine. ''First on the list. In Aberdeen.''

He wrote that night and within a week he had a reply, offering him the job! At the same time, however, he inserted an advert of his own, specifying his interest in the north east of Scotland. Several dentists replied, offering him work in Peterhead, Buckie, Stonehaven. Obviously he would be able to find work in the area, which was reassuring.

The next quandary was whether to settle on a job and hope to find a house nearby, or to find a house first. And there was also the question of selling our Northern Ireland house. Always providing that anyone would be interested in buying a house in Northern Ireland in those days. Would it be best to sell that first and see how much we got for it? Then we would know what we could afford in Scotland.

We put Lisbrega on the market in mid-September and were relieved to find there was immediate interest. Several people came to view it and then, as is the custom of house purchase there, they put in bids with the lawyer, bidding against each other. The reserve figure we had decided upon was soon passed and still the people who wanted the house continued to raise the price.

It was not easy to sit back and watch it happen, but I was seeing God's hand in it so I felt much more at peace than David who was tormented by all kinds of worries. Would the buyers all lose interest and stop bidding? When would it be right to close the deal? We were not looking for huge profits, but we knew that Scottish house prices were likely to be much higher than the Irish ones - as indeed they were. Would we be able to afford to buy a house over there?

At this point he asked yet again the recurring question: Do you think we are doing the right thing?

David was lying in bed and I was getting undressed. I didn't often talk to him openly about God and the way I was learning to rely on him in every situation. David had his own way of thinking and he left me free to have mine. But at that moment I felt I should make my position clear.

"Right - I'll tell you it my way, just once," I said. "You might not agree, but please just listen. I believe God wants us to go. I think he said it through Willie. He's given us plenty of interest in our house, and within a week you had a job offered just where we were thinking of going. Everything will be all right, if we just trust God."

David was silent for a while, obviously thinking.

"I hope you're right," he said, pulling the quilt round about his shoulders as he turned over to sleep.

After about two weeks of this see-saw tension - which felt like a much longer period - the lawyer finally phoned with an offer which he thought was the best he could get. He advised us to accept it and we did. Now, with our house provisionally sold, we were free to explore the Scottish part of the operation.

Early in October, David took a week off work and we travelled to Scotland for the third time that year. We would have five working days there - and we had quite a shopping list! We needed a job, a house and schools for the children, and especially somewhere suitable for James.

We left Paul and Helen under the supervision of friends, James in Greystone Hall and took Alison with us, as we set out on our daunting task.

Not surprisingly, David was plagued with nerves the whole time. How could we possibly find a job and somewhere to live in such a short space of time? And what if we couldn't find anywhere to live, would we be able to afford lodgings? And what about the cost of storing our furniture? Jobs seemed fairly plentiful, but which would be the right one? And, underlying it all, was the secret fear that something would go wrong with the house sale in Northern Ireland.

We were fortunate to be able to base ourselves again in Forfar and leave Alison with Granny when we went to the first job interviews.

We drove to Aberdeen on a day such as the north

east of Scotland often enjoys in autumn - very cold, with bright blue skies and sunshine which sets the grey granite buildings a-sparkle. David had two interviews in Aberdeen - one with the man who had made the first offer at the outset of our quest. I sat outside in the car praying and enjoying the prospect of late roses blooming in long beds at the side of the road. Both men offered him work - the choice was his to consider.

"Next stop the house agent's," I said. Using our new road map, we navigated our way through the unfamiliar streets to his office.

He had not very much to offer. The discovery of offshore oil was rapidly turning Aberdeen into a boom city and properties were snapped up as soon as they came on to the market. And as it was a University city, students filled most of the available flats.

"If you wanted to live outside Aberdeen in one of the villages down the coast, you might find something."

As it happened David had arranged a third interview for that evening with a dentist in Stonehaven, fifteen miles south of Aberdeen. Might there be any property there, we asked?

"There's just one old house which has been on the market for ages," the agent said. "I'll give you the prospectus." And he handed us a sheet of paper with details of a double fronted, typically Scottish house.

"We might as well go and look at it, seeing we'll be in Stonehaven anyway," I suggested.

David had arranged to meet the dentist when he finished work at eight o'clock, so we made an appointment to view the house at seven. The owner, Mr. McLean, a burly man who had been a Clyde pilot in his younger days, showed us round without making many comments.

A cold, dark evening is not the ideal time to see a house to its best advantage, especially when it is lit with 40 watt bulbs and strewn with dark, heavy, old-fashioned furniture.

But as soon as I went in, I felt instinctively that it was a 'good' house. A homely house, with distinct possibilities. When we had tramped through it, Mr. McLean took us out of the back door and, in the light of his feeble torch, we could just make out a walled garden with trees here and there.

"We'll think about it," David promised, as we left to keep our other appointment.

As I sat in the car in the square at Stonehaven while the temperature dropped to well below freezing, I asked the Lord whether this was the place he wanted us to live. No answer came, beyond a peace in trusting that he would guide us and there was no need to worry.

But worry kept David awake all that night. He tossed and turned and felt most unwell by the next morning.

One thing at least was clear. He would not be taking the job in Stonehaven because the premises were not ready for a second dentist to start work. And he needed to be able to start work immediately. He would have to choose between the Aberdeen jobs.

"Are we mad?" David asked anxiously as we set off on the almost fifty mile drive north to Aberdeen again next day.

"Not at all," I said as calmly as I could. "It's right."

In the near distance the Angus hills rimmed the horizon, reminding me of words I had read earlier in my Bible. I would try to hang on to their truth, for both of us. 'I lift up my eyes to the hills. From whence does my help come? My help comes from the Lord...' (Psalm 121).

I was relying on him to help in very practical ways and the more David leaned on me psychologically, the more I found I had to lean on the Lord. But the psalm which started with those hopeful words, ended with an even more strengthening promise: 'The Lord will keep your going out and your coming in from this time forth and for evermore'.

Going out and coming in seemed to describe our situation so well. So what was there to worry about, I asked myself, if I really was trusting that promise. Nothing - not houses, jobs, schools or anything - as long as I was taking God at his Word. It was even exciting, if a bit scary, to wonder just how he was going to bring it all about!

We looked at one or two more properties in the Aberdeen area that day. The only one that was at all suitable was really out of our price range so we asked for time to consider. When we enquired again a few hours later, it was sold. We decided to view the Stonehaven house again, in daylight.

Again I sensed the welcoming feel of the four, well-proportioned square rooms with their decorated, corniced ceilings. The four bedrooms and a box-room upstairs would give us all room to spread ourselves, and there were two bathrooms. Off the kitchen a small room, lined with shelves made what had once been a maid's bedroom into a fine pantry - we would have plenty of storage space. Four stone built sheds formed part of the garden wall - more storage space! - and a garage divided the small front garden from the more secluded and larger back one.

Again I had the feeling of 'rightness' and again I kept quiet, hoping David would sense it himself. If he took the Aberdeen job and we bought a house in Stonehaven he would have to travel back and forth every day. He was best able to judge how he would feel about that.

On the drive back to Forfar he made a suggestion. "Let's bring my parents to see the house tomorrow. If they think it's a good buy ..."

"Good idea," I agreed, feeling for my normally decisive husband. If only he could get a good night's sleep! But again he tossed and sighed, so I started to enumerate to him all the good points of the Stonehaven house. It was well-built, within easy walking distance of both the schools and the shops. We'd have to get rid of some of the dark brown varnish and maybe put in some more effective heating, but it was empty and available for immediate occupation and it cost less than we were selling Lisbrega for.

Before we set out on our hundred mile round trip with Granny and Grandpa next morning, I read my Daily Light and my Bible reading for the day, hoping for clues as to God's will, but I found nothing.

Pitneil, the house in Stonehaven, was already beginning to feel like home as we entered the double porch for the third time. I could tell that Granny liked it; it was her kind of house, and David's father also approved. Once we knew we were all in agreement we felt we should go ahead.

Mr. McLean and David agreed on a price and

then did what was customary in Scotland - they shook hands, and the deal was made.

Having been in Scotland for only a few days we had no business contacts whatsoever, but a phone call sufficed to obtain an appointment that morning with Mr. McLean's lawyer where David signed the schedule. All he had to do was to write at the foot of the schedule 'I accept your offer' and sign it. This made the agreement legally binding on both parties. There is no gazumping in Scotland!

It meant that Mr. McLean was thereafter obliged to sell us the property at the agreed price, and we were equally bound to complete the purchase. Either party could sue the other for failing to keep their side of the bargain. If only we could have been so sure of the sale of our Irish property!

Excitement tinged with apprehension gripped me at the way things were suddenly moving so rapidly. Surely it was going to be all right? I would have loved even a small indication from the Lord.

What possible connection could a postal strike have with all these events? God weaves some unusual details into the fabric of our lives which can so easily go unnoticed! It was because of a postal strike that I had brought my collection of used postage stamps with me so as to deliver them in person to the Christian Literature Crusade's Aberdeen bookshop. So, while David and his father kept their appointment with the solicitor, my mother-in-law and I walked down Union Street to the CLC shop.

While I was waiting to hand the stamps over, Granny caught sight of some small booklets she fancied and she bought a couple. "They'll come in handy for reading aloud at the Guild," she told me as we walked back to the car.

It was still very cold and we were glad to sit in the car's warmth again. Granny took out one of her booklets and started to read. It had an entry for each of thirty one days and, because it was the fourteenth of October, she turned to the fourteenth day. After just a few minutes she held it out to me.

"Read that," she said. "And put it on the steering wheel for those men."

More than a little surprised by her uncharacteristic action, I took the booklet and began to read.

"Perhaps there has arisen in your life a situation of great importance. You have looked to the Lord for direction and, assured of his divine leading, you have no doubt about the ultimate issues of that step. Our enemy is always watchful for opportunities to unsettle us, especially when he sees us stepping out on God's promises, and this is just the time when he will whisper his doubts in our ears. Let us not listen to his voice, but *go forward with confidence*, resting on this wonderful promise: 'Hath he said and shall he not do it?' (Numbers 23.19)''

Joy surged through me. God hadn't let me down! In his own time and in his own way, he had given me his confirmation. Unmistakably!

There is even a sequel to that little episode, for when we had been back in Ireland just two days, the phone rang. It was Marjorie, a Christian friend.

"Betty, I've a message for you,'' she said. "The other day John was reading this wee booklet. And he pointed to one page and said, 'You should tell that to Betty McKay'. I've got it here and I'll read it now.''

Incredibly she started: "Perhaps there has arisen in your life ...''

"Thanks Marjorie,'' I interrupted. "You'll never believe it, but I read that. Tell John that I got the message the very day I needed it.'' And I went on to explain to her what had happened. We were both amazed at the way God had contrived to use the same, undated booklet, through two totally unconnected people, to get his message to me - in duplicate!

David and his father returned within the hour, having completed the house purchase, arranged a mortgage, insurance, everything. We could speed down the road to Forfar with a sense of accomplishment, relief ... and wonderment.

That evening David phoned one of the dentists

and accepted the job, agreeing to start in early November. So we had a house, a job and the prospect of schools. The only thing we had not had time to do was inquire about a place for James.

But our heavenly Father had that in hand too. That Thursday evening the Kirk elder called with Granny's communion cards. This in itself was unusual because he normally just posted them through the letterbox. This time he came in and, as they chatted together, we discovered that he was the Education Officer in the Angus region. He promised to contact his opposite number in the Kincardine area and ask him to find a place for James.

If nothing could be found locally, he said, James might have to go to a Centre in another part of Scotland, possibly Glasgow. I didn't like the sound of that, but it was just something else to trust the Lord for. And hadn't we had ample proof of his ability and care during the past few days?

We sailed back to Ireland next day leaving a somewhat reluctant Alison with Granny. The next few weeks would be a hectic process of sorting, throwing out and packing, as well as making a round of goodbye calls, and if Alison were with Granny it would be a help.

In spite of David's fears, the sale of Lisbrega went through without a hitch.

On Friday the 29th October I collected James from Greystone Hall for the last time. All his pals, including his sparring partners, Alec and Ian, lined up with Mr. Carrington to say goodbye as we drove away.

James waved back happily. Did he realise that he would probably never see them again? Or was it just the part of him that still happily accepts everything as it comes, helping him look forward without fear to whatever life in Scotland would hold?

CHAPTER SEVEN

A Taste Of Scotland

Two men loaded our motley collection of worldly goods into a big blue container as we worked in Lisbrega's empty shell, making it as clean as possible under the circumstances.

As I stood and looked around the upstairs lounge for the last time, I remembered the latest of God's lovely touches on our leaving.

Just a few days earlier we had had a most unexpected visit from a couple of missionary friends. On leave from Kenya and quite unaware of our plans to move, Dick and Joan had called in to see us.

"I should like to ask the Lord's blessing on your move," Dick said just before they left. "Would you mind?"

And he had done just that as the four of us stood with bowed heads in the lounge. It was the end of one stage and the beginning of a new one. And the Lord would be with us. I was very grateful for that strengthening thought.

When we had done all we could in the house our

friends, the Lynns, took us to their home where we shared a lovely meal before driving the thirty or so miles to Larne and the ferry which took us across the sea to Stranraer.

Once in Scotland we drove for a while along the dark, deserted November roads then pulled our caravanette into the lay-by, made up the beds and tried to snatch some sleep.

Much later that day, Thursday the fourth of November, we arrived at Granny's for the fourth time in 1971. James and Alison were overjoyed to see each other again and before long they settled down to a game of Snakes and Ladders.

"We'll have an early start tomorrow," we told Granny. "The men said the container would be in Stonehaven at eight o'clock."

We managed to arrive before it and the bare wooden floor-boards echoed as the four children explored all the new rooms for the first time.

"I want this bedroom," Paul shouted from upstairs, claiming one of the front bedrooms which overlooked the street. We had chosen the other. The girls decided to share one of the back rooms for a start and we gave the other back one to James for his own.

That was one of the good things about moving to Scotland. James would be able to live at home again; our family could be all together. At least, we hoped so. That was just one of the myriad enquiries we had to make.

Bare boards we might have on the floor and camping style meals on the table, but I determined that, on that first Sunday, we would all go to church. David came too.

We had heard that there were several churches in Stonehaven - no fewer than three were Church of Scotland - more or less the same as the Presbyterian churches we had attended in Northern Ireland. Only four, rather grand, houses separated us along Bath Street, from Fetteresso Church, so we went there on that first Sunday.

On succeeding Sundays we did try other churches, but we finally settled in Fetteresso. Helen joined the Bible class which was held before the morning service and James and Alison attended Primary Sunday School together.

The next day, Monday, while James and I continued the mammoth task of unpacking cardboard boxes of crockery and foodstuffs and deciding where they would best fit into our newly washed shelves and cupboards, David went the rounds of the schools and got Paul and Helen installed at the Mackie Academy. Then he delivered Alison to Arduthie Primary School.

Before the week was out Mr. Cardno from the Stonehaven Education Department, called to see us. His colleague in Forfar had contacted him as promised and, after chatting to us about James, he arranged an appointment for us to go and see Mrs. Innes, Headmistress of Beechwood School in Aberdeen.

Beechwood stands in rising wooded grounds, not far from the Aberdeen Royal Infirmary. David, James and I went there one afternoon and the Headmistress interviewed us and showed us round some of the classrooms.

"We have all sorts of children here," she explained. "Some are mentally handicapped, some physically and some a combination of both. We also take in disturbed children who are proving difficult to handle in the normal schools. So we're quite a mixture. But I think you'll find James will settle down nicely with us after a while."

I sincerely hoped he would. But I guessed that, with his gentle, inoffensive nature, he might find Beechwood hard going. I consoled myself with the knowledge that at least he'd be home every evening and I would know if all was going well.

Once the arrangements were made, a taxi picked him up every morning at 8.15 and brought him home again at 3.45. Typically, James never made any protest about going in the taxi each morning, but gradually I developed a special sense so that I could discern when things were upsetting him. I learned not to ignore little remarks like: "She wasn't very kind to me."

If I followed them up with gentle, relaxed questions, I might discover that one of the girls in the taxi had tugged out chunks of his hair, or scratched his face. From other equally casual comments, I discovered how much James loved the lady taxi driver who was on duty most days. What a time she must have had driving to Aberdeen with four mentally handicapped children and no escort!

Most children find new schools difficult at first and ours all re-acted differently to the settling-in period. Having been taught only 'traditional' maths, Paul had to switch over to the new system and prepare to sit exams for Highers within the next five or six months. So it was nose to the grindstone for him, but he made it and even won a bursary.

Helen's gregarious nature soon provided her with a group of friends and, as she had no major exams in the offing, she seemed to fit in with the rest without any great problems.

Alison had greater difficulty in making the change. Having progressed according to ability in the Irish system, she was two years in advance of her Scottish peers and the Headmaster wisely recommended that she move back at least one year to P5. Even so, she was always a year younger than the other pupils in her class. Scholastically she coped without problem. But one or two of the tougher girls made playtimes and the walks home from school a misery. Alison didn't complain to me so I only found out from a neighbour that one of the girls was demanding ten pence each from Alison and her friend so that they could walk home unmolested!

She was not happy with her teacher either. When I asked around, I discovered that the woman had had a rather unhappy life and was coping with a recent bereavement. People also questioned whether she was particularly suited to teaching. I explained some of this to Alison to help her understand and we prayed together, asking God to comfort the lady and make her into a happier person. Alison's attitude was significantly better after our prayer, and she gradually settled down.

James must have also noticed a great change in the school system, though he was not able to articulate it to anybody.

There seems to be a natural resentment in some children to anybody who is different and new, and something of this came out through in nick-names. In Greystone Hall James had been 'Pie' - because he loved food of all kinds and would often pop into the kitchen there to see what the cook might have to offer! - though no-one would ever have guessed from his skinny frame that he had such a fondness for food. But at Beechwood James was given the name 'IRA', which he hated. Had we been more alert, other boys' nicknames like 'Bulldog' and 'Police dog' might have hinted at the bullying which sometimes went on in the playground.

For us the most distressing incident was when James came home with a nasty burn on his leg. He didn't mention it at first, but when he took his socks off at bedtime, I was horrified.

"How did that happen?" I asked when I saw the angry, red sore.

"Some boys held me down in the playground" was all he said. It took a few minutes more to elicit that, while one boy had sat on top of him, another had held a piece of glass and focused the sun's rays on to James' flesh until it burnt. The staff were also distressed when we reported it to them, but they had an unenviable task with such large numbers of children and only a few staff available to supervise the playground.

On the positive side James enjoyed some of the new activities he started at Beechwood. He did painting, some metalwork and basketry - though he wasn't very good at it. His stiff fingers found it difficult to control the canes and he would end up with a spoiled basket. I still have one successful basket in which I keep my Christmas writing materials. I also have - and use - a small, polished wooden tray which James made at Beechwood.

James took great pride in making all these useful things. But he completely mystified me for a moment with one of his announcements.

"Guess what I'm making for you now, Mum? A fish lice." A picture of fish covered in ghastly creepy-crawlies instantly flashed into my mind.

"A what?" I squeaked in horror. Then, realising, I said more approvingly; "I think you mean a fish *slice*."

"Yes - a fish lice," James nodded, happy that I had finally understood. And of course the perforated metal tool he eventually brought home remained exactly that; our fish lice!

Then there was riding. On Thursdays a group of children went out to riding stables in the country at Tertowie. They had special instructors and equipment and without a doubt those simple riding lessons were for James the highlight of his time at Beechwood.

To our great delight and astonishment James also learned to swim at Beechwood. Swimming had long been one of our favourite family activities. In a way we were together, yet each one had freedom to do their own thing, once they could swim well enough. Winter and summer we had made use of the lovely indoor pools in Northern Ireland and James enjoyed splashing about as much as anyone. But in spite of all our efforts we had never managed to teach him to swim. Once in the water, every muscle in his body seemed to tense up, and even for me to pull his arms through the swimming strokes was like trying to move the limbs of a stiff wooden puppet.

I have no idea how they managed it, but Beechwood had its own learner's pool and one day James assured us that he really could swim. Needless to say we had to see to believe, but it was quite true.

So once again new life patterns began to emerge for each of us. Part of this pattern was our attendance at Fetteresso church, where David and Paul were soon co-opted into the choir and I into teaching in Sunday School. Unfortunately David became disillusioned with some aspects of the church and began to spend more and more of his Sundays working in his very demanding garden. Doubts took over once again.

Shortly after we moved, I had more or less issued a spiritual challenge to Paul and Helen. I felt that in Northern Ireland they had often gone along to things because, as my children, it was expected of them. So in Stonehaven I told them: ''You're new here. Nobody knows anything about you. You can go to whatever activities you want.''

Naturally I hoped they would link themselves

with some Christian group beyond church, but at fourteen and sixteen I felt they were old enough to exercise their own judgment. It would be a good test of their earlier training and commitment, because, by that time, they had both asked Jesus to be their Saviour.

Only days later Paul said he was going to a Scripture Union meeting at lunchtime. He'd seen a boy wearing an SU badge and had asked about it - so he'd been invited along. Helen joined the girls' group. She particularly enjoyed the Friday night meetings held in the leader's home. There would come a time later on when this independent teenager would rebel at some of the things 'Jennifer said', and I would have to quietly point out that when 'Jennifer said' things, she was only passing on what Jesus taught or spoke out against.

For some months the house itself swallowed up most of my time. We had central heating installed downstairs, which meant total upheaval in the kitchen especially. Gas men, electricians, joiners, painters and plumbers seemed to come and go in never ending succession, most of them appreciating regular cups of tea or coffee and what home bakes I could rustle up.

Food shopping trips forced me to go out at least occasionally, and I enjoyed taking different routes to the town centre which was just a five minute walk

- on the way there! Coming back up the steep brae took longer and I soon decided that a shopping trolley was a must.

I was always fascinated by the variety of houses in Stonehaven. Whenever I went out I noticed another one at an unusual angle, or a half hidden garden. I often felt actively happy walking along the Stonehaven streets with their frequent glimpses of the sea in all its moods. I was very grateful to God for bringing us here.

My daily time with him was especially precious because I had no other adult Christian friend at the start. Church was the place you went to worship, but the weather was what most people seemed to talk about afterwards, if they stopped to talk at all.

But one day a young woman rang our doorbell. She had a little girl beside her, a collecting tin in her hand, and a very apologetic look on her face.

"I wonder if you'd like to give anything for the Bible Society?" she asked quietly.

So many charities clamour for our help and I am sometimes chary of supporting one of two of them, but about the Bible Society I had no such hesitation.

My 'Oh yes - gladly' was obviously a relief to her for she smiled most warmly. We chatted for several minutes on the doorstep and she invited me to go and have coffee with her one morning.

I felt a glow of excitement as I went inside. "I

bet she's a Christian,'' I thought, suddenly realising how much I was missing my Irish Christian friends and the way we'd been able to meet and talk things through together. It would be so lovely to have a Christian friend again, I thought. Why had it never occurred to me to pray for one?

The young woman, Meg Duncan, had felt the same vibes. She went and phoned one of her friends: ''I'm sure the woman who's come to live in Pitneil is a Christian,'' she said.

When I went for coffee a few days later, we confirmed our suspicions and experienced that wonderful, no-barrier, instant rapport which only Jesus can give. That morning we unwittingly sowed the seeds of a women's Bible study group which was to see many different women, and their toddling children, come together and grow in Christ. Some have gone on to start other groups, even in far away places, while always leaving a core group which, by God's grace, still continues.

Meg also told me of a monthly fellowship of men and women from different churches who met in one home or another to study the Bible and spend time together. I became part of this group too, another group which, by God's grace, would evolve into a weekly after-church meeting, and slowly change and develop as healthy, growing things will, affecting the lives of all the men and women

- and later young people - who attended. It all seemed to be part of God's continuing confirmation of the rightness of our move to Stonehaven.

The timing of our move also coincided with another of our previous interests. About three years earlier, Paul and I had started to learn Braille under the auspices of the Torch Trust for the Blind. Once we had completed the course and passed an examination set by the Royal National Institute for the Blind, we began to work together at transcribing Christian books into Braille for Torch's lending library.

Only a few months after we arrived in Stonehaven, the founders of Torch Trust, Mr. and Mrs. Heath, came to Aberdeen, hoping to form a local Torch group for the benefit of blind and partially sighted people living in the area. Naturally we were interested. We'd never actually met anyone connected with Torch. All our work had been done through the post. So we attended the meeting and - surprise, surprise! - we were co-opted on to a Committee, as were most of the folk who attended that first event.

A monthly Saturday afternoon meeting came into being with more and more visually handicapped people and their friends attending. James came along too and quickly fitted in in an amazing way. He was the one who noticed if anyone was without a song book and he would go and get one. He became very good a guiding people to their seats and moving obstacles out of their way. He helped to serve the refreshments, and to clear up later on. He loved to lift the offering too, and would jingle the collecting bag in front of the ones who couldn't see, so that they knew the bag had reached them.

I'm sure that it was the fact that he was learning to use his own handicap in whatever way he could that made him so well accepted and even popular at Torch. Many a one told me how much they loved to hear him call out his name at the roll call, saying proudly: "James McKay, Stonehaven."

This is another meeting which still continues, though for some years now other activities have prevented us from going. But it gave James his first taste of fairly independent public service, and it helped us realise how much he loves to contribute.

In August 1973 David changed his job again, though this time the change did not involve the rest of the family in any upheaval. He moved out of private practice and became a School Dental Officer based in Banchory, thirteen miles inland from Stonehaven.

Not long after this we discovered that God had yet again been working in advance to meet James' need in an amazing way. He did it through Geoffrey and Margaret Saunders, a couple who first discerned the need of mentally handicapped children in the area and then worked devotedly to do what they could to meet that need.

They began by forming a branch of the Scottish Society for the Mentally Handicapped - SSMH. Mrs. Saunders was a founder member and welfare officer for the group, and her husband became Chairman three years later. The small group of concerned people included Miss Mary Mann, Matron of Keith Lodge, the Church of Scotland Home for Handicapped Children in Stonehaven. This embryo Day Centre first met in a room in Keith Lodge with four 'students' under sixteen. Later they moved to the village hall at Muchalls, a nearby coastal village, and finally moved to an old domestic science room at Portlethen school, just a few miles outside Stonehaven.

All the time, the members of this somewhat migrant group were urging the authorities to do more towards the education of these children with special needs. Years of effort, largely inspired by the Saunders, were rewarded when the purpose-built Carronhill Special School was finally built in Stonehaven in 1973.

Once open, it was still an uphill struggle to keep the school going, and it was very much dependent on the generosity of local people who responded to the various money raising efforts, such as the annual Autumn Fayre. Rotary, Round Table and many other organisations all made contributions, perhaps the most touching being £25 raised by four little girls from Newtonhill who collected as many items as they could (using a go-kart!) and held a sale in their local hall.

The first Headmaster of Carronhill School was Mr. Robbie. He had been one of James' teachers at Beechwood and James was sorry to see him leave there. He would miss him.

But not for long. Once Carronhill was opened, James was accepted as a pupil. At fourteen, he was the oldest one there, and the tallest. Right from the start he loved it. The small numbers and very high teacher-pupil ratio meant a much less stressful atmosphere and James thrived.

Because the school was about a mile away, James could have been collected from home by taxi as most of the younger ones were. But Mr. Robbie felt it would foster James' independence if he could get there by his own efforts.

For several months James had been riding a bicycle and he seemed quite proficient, though just occasionally his road sense would lapse dangerously. But Mr. Robbie was keen for him to try to cycle to school, so we planned what we thought was the quietest route.

David and I walked him through this route the

evening before he was to make his first solo effort, but on the morning itself I chickened out and followed behind him on my own bike! I was glad I did. One crossroads, which had been quiet the evening before, was alive with cars coming and going in seemingly all directions, many of them stopping and opening their doors to disgorge children who were going to the school on the opposite corner. It was an eventuality we had quite overlooked. I shouted to James to dismount, and then walked him and his bike safely on to the quieter road. "Never again, James," I said. And we later worked out a less crowded route for him.

It was just another of the new experiences James was to have at Carronhill. In particular, he learned two new skills. One was cookery. On Fridays James would come home and carefully extract a well-wrapped, slightly-warm little parcel from his saddle-bag.

"Is this for me?" I would ask, admiring a pair of rather flat fruit scones, or some jammy buns.

"One of them is," James would say. "You can share it with Alison." And he would show me his recipe book, hand-written, where the first entry for any recipe was always: 1. Wash your hands.

We have quite a few musicians in our family, one or two with talent and the rest of us interested but willing plodders. So, not surprisingly, James was also interested. But, apart from letting him have a go at whatever instrument he fancied - piano, guitar, tin whistle - we had never considered that he might actually be able to learn to play any of them.

But he joined the music group at Carronhill and not only learned to play the recorder but also to read music! How he laughed when I tried to match the music on the sheet to the holes on a recorder, totally without success! And I was also able to use his ability to read music as another point of encouragement, for we had friends with University degrees who sang well, but couldn't read music!

This new achievement meant that he could now also try to play the piano from music, and he spent hours sitting patiently working out tunes. His pace was always his own, very slow, but how he enjoyed working at it!

James' sixteenth birthday was approaching, which meant he would be due to leave Carronhill. The problem was, what would he do then? There was absolutely no provision that we knew of. Would he have to spend the rest of his life at home with me? Or had God other plans?

"I always thought that we must be a special family because we had such a special brother." Alison, Madrid 1991

CHAPTER EIGHT

Hitherto The Lord Has Helped Us

"When you look back and see how specifically God has provided for James' needs all his life," I said to David one evening, "I can't believe he's going to stop now. I'm sure he'll have something. We just have to find out what it is."

David had grown used to my way of interpreting events, though I was never sure how far he went along with it. "I wonder if he could stay on a bit longer at Carronhill?" he mused. "Shall I ask Mr. Robbie?"

Mr. Robbie was sympathetic and suggested we write to the Education authorities. As the school was still below its full complement, they just might grant our request. They did! James was given one more year's grace, which eventually became two years. He was very conscious of being the oldest boy and I think his good, co-operative behaviour was an asset to the school, perhaps especially in the playground, where he would take it on himself to see there was no nonsense on the swings and other equipment. His adult size must have awed some of the wee ones.

In church too he had moved from Sunday School to Bible class. I'm not sure how much he understood, but he was always keen to go and occasionally he would come home and report that the leader had not been too well prepared that day! We were very grateful for the way he was accepted by everybody at church. He was made to feel he belonged, even though the other pupils in Bible class were a good few years younger.

God's immaculate timing next meant that, when James was seventeen, Mr. Robbie began to cast around for local firms who might offer work experience to pupils about to leave. James was one of the candidates.

The idea was that they would work for one or two weeks in a real work situation. The firm concerned would have to provide someone to work alongside and supervise them, and the Government would reimburse them for the time thus lost.

James had a period at a Fun Food Factory, which he enjoyed because on Fridays he was given a bag of cream-filled buns to bring home! Then he did a stint in our local supermarket, where he managed to put wrong prices on several tins of carrots! And finally he spent a few weeks in a local garage where the elderly owner took a very caring interest in him and presented him with a nice new anorak when he left.

It was all good experience, and James' personal relationships were very good in each place. People who met him at that time still greet him on the street.

But the fact was that he would not have been able to work effectively in any of those situations. And his eighteenth birthday was fast approaching when he would be out of the Education Authority's care.

It was at that time of crisis that God saw to it that another job opportunity materialised.

"I'm going to Woodcot Hospital, Mum," James announced one day, from his kitchen rocking chair vantage point. He and David had constructed the chair for my birthday and James made a bee-line for it every day as soon as he came home. Then our huge, black, long-haired cat - called Snowball - would just as surely make a bee-line for James' knee and after 'nosing' him for a while, would drape himself over James' long legs while James started to caress him with long, slow strokes. Snowball was a stray who adopted us and James loved his company.

"Woodcot? What for?"

"I'm going to be a hospital porter. It's work experience."

Woodcot was the local geriatric hospital and about the same distance from home as Carronhill.

James' initial two weeks became three, then four and in the end he was offered permanent, part-time employment as a porter.

His job included emptying bins, collecting dirty laundry, delivering clean laundry, distributing stores and - the job he came to hate most - cleaning the car park. How he loathed picking up cigarette ends!

I noticed that he was often quite tired when he came home, though a cup of coffee and a seat worked wonders.

On occasions he would pour out a string of complaints about the things that had been said or done to him. I was glad to be available as a safety valve - and I learned a lot too! He especially resented being asked to do something that was not on his list.

"That's *his* job," he would rage. "It's not mine. He just wants me to do all the dirty work. I nearly said to him ..." And he would go off into a long tirade of all the things which had obviously been burning inside him.

"Tomorrow I shall tell him ..." but of course, he never did. We are not a family of confronters, so James had absolutely no training. I could imagine him working away, staying silent under criticism, only the lowered brows betraying his hurt or annoyance.

Perhaps some of the criticism was valid, for

James was not a very enthusiastic worker, as we found whenever we set him to mow the lawn. After the first few swathes he would disappear to watch television, or sit on the low garden wall and watch the world go by. He had often to be prodded quite a bit to finish the job, so maybe the folk at Woodcot had their complaints about him too.

One man seemed to give him particular problems so I tried to find out more. It transpired that the man was quite elderly and suffered from asthma - perhaps he was barely fit to work. No wonder he could sometimes be crotchety. When I explained the man's difficulty to James it made a big difference and James offered him extra help. To understand is to forgive, they say.

"Shall we pray for him?"

I had popped into James' bedroom on my own way to bed - partly because I could hear a voice as I passed his door and was curious. I'd listened for a few minutes until it stopped, then gone in.

"Who were you talking to?"

"I was just praying." So I sat on the bed and we prayed for his colleague too.

After that I often cocked my ear as I passed his door, not eavesdropping, but amazed at the length of time he lay there in the dark, just talking to God, praying for the family, his grandparents and other people he knew.

James worked at Woodcot for four and a half years. He received wages - though not so much as he would have been paid on Social Security! He enjoyed the status of having a job, and never demurred about going, but I suspect he was never really happy there. Still, as it was mornings only, it seemed preferable to staying at home with nothing specific to do. And we felt it was good that he was learning to hold his own in a work situation which was fairly sheltered.

Tension sometimes showed itself in the same old way - a tell-tale damp patch at the front of his trousers would betray him. "James, why didn't you go to the toilet sooner?" I couldn't always keep the exasperation from my voice. The truth was that he hadn't dared to absent himself from his task to go.

I was glad for James that he had an afternoon activity too. It helped release some of this unfortunate tension.

As on so many occasions in the past, God had been preparing this activity so that it was available at just the right time. Again he had used the Saunders, the same couple who had worked so hard to start Carronhill. Under the auspices of the Scottish Society for the Mentally Handicapped (SSMH) they had next turned their attention to providing something to occupy mentally handicapped adults, as a follow-on from Carronhill.

In order to prove to the authorities that there was a genuine need for a special centre, they had hired rooms in the local Community Centre and begun to run classes-cum-workshops on a voluntary basis. Their aim was that the authorities should provide an adult training centre but, as a stop-gap until that could materialise, they had gathered six men and four women trainees and made a start.

Together with one or two staff and some voluntary helpers, the trainees had learnt to make a variety of articles: knitted dishcloths, covered coathangers and some brightly-coloured, ingeniously devised dollies made of circles of cotton, stitched and strung together on elastic.

As time went on they had extended their range to include leather, woodwork and other goods. From time to time they had held sales of their products in order to get funds to buy more materials.

Their greatest expense had been paying for the trainees to be transported to and from the centre each day. All money had to be raised by special events or as charity gifts, and although local people supported them generously, funds were often very low.

It was this centre, less than five minutes' walking distance from home, that James started to attend in the afternoons. There was absolutely no pressure and he fitted in very happily right from the start.

After many delays and much pressure from the SSMH and the Saunders, the authorities finally built Forest View Centre for Mentally Handicapped Adults. It had space for 60 trainees and would serve a wide area. It opened in July 1980 and James transferred there along with the rest of the trainees. He still spent his mornings at Woodcot but he went from there to Forest View for his lunch and the rest of the day.

I was not surprised that he was happy at Forest View. On one of the open days, James proudly showed us round the attractive one-storey building standing in well-laid-out grounds. As he led us from room to room I noticed the pleasant colour schemes and the attractive curtains everywhere. We saw the metal work room, the woodwork department where James spent part of his time; the training kitchen, the dining room with its own coffee bar where trainees learned to serve each other.

Next he took us to the Area for Daily Living where trainees were taught housekeeping and some of the other skills they would need for independent adult living such as bedmaking, and basic cookery. The scope of activities at the centre continued to evolve, expanding and contracting with changes in Government policy, but the main aim has increasingly been to encourage trainees to become as independent as possible.

For James, this pattern of divided days continued until the summer of 1982. We occasionally questioned whether he should carry on working at Woodcot. Yet would it not be a retrograde step for him to move into the Centre full-time?

I think it was steady prayer which opened my eyes to see the next step, through James himself. At Woodcot he was allocated two weeks holiday. In practice this just meant two weeks of mornings at home.

James had a better idea. "Couldn't I go to the Centre all day on my holidays?" His voice showed pleasure at the prospect.

The Centre manager was quite happy for James to do this and by the end of the first week I noticed a significant change in him. He was much more relaxed, no longer tired by tea time - and no wet pants! The unexpected experiment convinced me that, backward step or not, James' place was at the Centre.

He became a full-time trainee in 1982. This meant he could join in the whole range of projects and activities in the areas of both work and sport.

He began to take part in swimming events, learnt to play pool, draughts and dominoes. He also became a very enthusiastic member of the football team as well as playing darts and carpet bowls. He was helped to develop a reasonable skill as a photographer and encouraged to play his recorder and his keyboard.

He also attempted quite a range of work assignments. He spent several terms in the woodwork department, sanding, polishing and varnishing a variety of chairs and tables - all too often his shirt as well! He enjoyed woodwork and, when the woodwork department closed, he started to attend an evening woodwork class instead.

He helped in the Printing Department too, printing tickets for various functions. He spent a term in the cement section, helping to make bird baths and garden gnomes amongst other things. All these departments have now been closed down.

His favourite work was in the garden section where he would weed, water and prick out tiny plants.

These gradual changes in James' life pattern took place against changes for the rest of the family as, one by one, they left home.

Helen was the first to go. In 1976, during her second year at Teacher Training College, she moved into Aberdeen. James missed her. She was always fun to have around, helping him to knit, sending him on errands to buy illicit cigarettes and rewarding him with a share which they both kept a secret from me. He was glad to see her whenever she turned up at weekends or went on holiday with us.

Paul left home to be married in September 1979, having qualified MA PhD at Aberdeen University. I would suspect that James hardly missed Paul - though he happily took over his bedroom! Their lives never had much in common and I think James was always rather in awe of him. They were too un-alike to make real contact, though there was no conflict.

Alison also moved into Aberdeen in 1979 where she was reading French and Spanish at University. Her relationship with James was motherly, almost akin to my own. James reciprocated her love, though he too recognized its nature. She once drew up a much needed personal hygiene plan for him and he agreed to it all. In fact, he didn't change a single habit! Typically he would agree to any suggestion, but then do exactly as he pleased!

Apart from the weekends when Alison came home, James was reduced to our company. But it all happened gradually and his own life and work probably compensated or any sense of loss, and we settled down to our ménage à trois very happily.

James attended the Centre every day and when he came home, he would sit in the rocking chair and pour out stories of what he had been doing, or com-plain about the behaviour of some of the trainees.

One in particular was the bane of his life. I would listen for what I thought was a reasonable time, but then I steered the conversation away from that particular person. I felt it was right to let James get rid of his annoyance, but wrong to let this other person spoil the rest of his evening.

This stage highlighted one factor which has been missing throughout James' life. With the possible exception of his time at Greystone Hall, James had no friends. The districts we lived in had few children and, in any case, James was away at school. Even when we moved to Scotland the children at Beechwood and Carronhill were drawn from a wide area and not available as local friends. Perhaps this was why he was sometimes known as a loner at the Centre.

Yet he was also gregarious and enjoyed the company of other people. We were always grateful for the way our own friends made him welcome - though when people didn't invite him specifically, I hated to ask. It seemed like asking a favour which they might find awkward to refuse. I was grateful for the way he was accepted by people at church where he always felt welcome. Even there I think he was seen as part of our family rather than as a man who would value an offer of friendship in his own right.

It may be his natural reticence or perhaps part of

his disability that he would find it almost impossible to initiate a friendship himself, though he would respond warmly to any friendly overtures. Perhaps handicapped people in any church have a similar need.

But at least at church James felt free to volunteer his services and he was often able to be of real help setting up chairs for the evening service and handing out hymn books as people arrived. At our time of open prayer, James occasionally prayed. Usually briefly - always from the heart. Many people have said how much they have been moved by his simple, sincere prayers.

In 1981 David had a serious illness and spent several weeks in Aberdeen Royal Infirmary. This completely altered our life. Never a very confident driver, I was grateful to have James with me as we daily drove what became an all to familiar route into Aberdeen. I really valued his companionship. He was capable of sitting peaceably and companionably silent for quite long stretches, and was always content, just happy for us to be together. Without any exchange of words, I knew he knew how I was feeling. His could be a deeply comforting presence.

David eventually recovered and came home and the three of us settled back into our old pattern. We never thought that the Lord was planning yet another change in our lives, one which would concern James in particular.

~~~~~~

'James is always polite and ... willing to lend a helping hand.' James Maguire, Homemaker 1990

~~~~~~

CHAPTER NINE

In Everything . . .
God works for good with those who love him
(Romans 8:28 RSV)

"We're going to have a hostel."

James loved to have an important piece of news to share when he came home from the Centre. The SSMH had managed to persuade the local authority to build a new complex consisting of a hostel which could house twelve people, and two extra staff houses.

"Who's going to live in it?" I asked.

"We don't know yet."

It set us thinking though. I liked having James at home where I could look after him. I could see that a hostel might be welcome as a place for James to stay while we were on holiday, but I wasn't ready to part with him completely. So I was quite relieved when the twelve places were quickly filled by other people.

But once again, God was allowing the unsettling possibilities to prepare us gently for what he had in store for James. About twelve months later one of the staff houses was turned into a Group Home.

The idea was that four compatible trainees would learn to live together in the house and, with some initial assistance, move toward independent living. James was one of the first four people to be offered a place. The ball was in our court - what should we do?

Part of me still wanted him to live at home. How would he ever manage to do all his own cooking, shopping, washing, ironing, cleaning? How would he handle money? He'd never needed to before. I didn't think it would work at all.

But as David and I talked about it, I gradually saw that we had to think of James' long term future. We would not be there for ever - would it be right to keep him relying on us? Should we at least not let him try this opportunity of independent living?

Again I was forced back to Dr. Watt's words, spoken so long ago: It all depends on how long he goes on developing.

Was this to be another stage in his development? I finally consoled myself with the thought that we'd still be on hand to watch over what happened. If it didn't work out, he could always come back home.

James moved into the Group Home on the 6th January 1986.

During the Christmas and New Year holiday I

tried to be positive and build up a sense of anticipation. "You'll soon be in your lovely new house, James," I would encourage him. "And there'll be a nice warm bedroom ... not like here." Pitneil had no heating upstairs and the bedrooms in winter could be arctic, with ice *in*side the windows sometimes.

Another man, Roddy, and two young women moved into the bungalow with James. They had three bedrooms, a large living room, bathroom and a dining kitchen, attractively furnished with a polished pine dresser and matching dining suite. It was equipped with a refrigerator and an automatic washing machine as well as crockery and cutlery. The bedrooms had matching sheets, pillow-cases and continental quilts and a lovely selection of towels.

They had certainly been given all the material essentials, I thought. But what about the four people? Would the experiment work for them?

At first an official helper was assigned to the group. She came in each morning to help them make breakfast and get them off to the Centre. She came again in the afternoon to help with the evening meal and the routine chores. The intention was that she would teach them how to do these things, but the first helper was so 'good-hearted' that she did most things for them, so the initial period of her help stretched on and on and they became very reliant on her.

James especially was very fond of this lady. Her accent was similar to my own and she gave him lots of quick cuddles. I really believe God provided this mother-figure to help James in his move away from home.

Both men soon settled into their new living pattern, but unfortunately the young women did not. They tended to stay locked in their shared bedroom, refusing to be part of communal living.

It was perhaps not surprising. They were four people from very different backgrounds, each with a handicap, who had been chosen to make the experiment of group living. James told us of a few stormy scenes when one of the women became noisy, abusive and even violent. After a few months both women left.

Peace reigned. James and Roddy got on well. A few months later another young man came to occupy the empty room. He was less able than the other two in some ways, so when they did their weekly shopping, he pushed the trolley while James and Roddy alternately read the shopping list and collected the goods or took charge of the cash. Their helper had earlier assisted them in planning a week's menus so they would know what to buy. Oven chips were high on the list!

They shared meal preparation and dishes and took turns at keeping the public part of the house clean. Each kept his own room tidy - in theory! You could be lucky to find a space to put your foot down on James' floor sometimes!

Then the latest young man decided to go back home to live, though he still attended the Centre.

James and Roddy were alone together again when the people in charge decided they should move into the same type of house next door so that the one they were living in could be adapted to accommodate a fresh intake of people, some of whom were in wheel chairs. By this time too, outside help was gradually phased out.

Roddy was the next to leave, though for a happier reason. His name came to the top of the housing list and he was given a council bungalow. Shortly afterwards he obtained permanent work with the Council and became completely independent. For Roddy the system had worked well.

This left James living on his own also for the next few months until two more men could be found who felt they might make a go of living in the house alongside him. Again, their handicaps were different - one was even tempered, the other much more volatile. Sometimes the arrangement seemed to be working, sometimes not. James found the quieter man compatible but unfortunately he left because of the too frequent violent and aggressive outbursts of the other. James and the second man are still together, living in a kind of uneasy truce.

It is hard to assess how well the experiment in group living is working. It seems to depend so much on the individuals. James and his present 'friend' share the same house, but live quite independently within it.

They make their own way to the Centre, shop for their own goods instead of having a common purse as at the start, and they cook separate evening meals. They both draw a weekly Disablement Pension and dispose of it in ways which they discuss with the Homemaker, as their particular Social Worker is called, though they each have the final say.

Both men usually spend the weekends with their parents, though James always goes back to his own home to sleep.

When James left home there was certainly a more tangible gap in our own lives than when any of the other children left. Suddenly, after thirty-one years, we were back to being a couple! I was grateful that we had always had a good relationship, but even so it felt strange not to have to consider a third person.

Certainly it gave us a new freedom - even to do simple things like taking a late evening stroll together, knowing there was no-one left behind in the house. But even freedom can require adjustment!

One of our daughters was pleased about this very aspect. She had seen what I had been unwilling to recognise: that, with James always around, there was a subtle difference in my relationship with David. I was 'in between' two people and inevitably, one got precedence. Often it was James.

"Dad needs to be first sometimes," she pointed out.

But for James, freedom brought other, unforeseen problems. He had a weakness for alcohol which he found hard to control. And when under the influence of drink he was easily drawn to the fruit machines which were so thoughtfully provided by hotelkeepers.

David had always been a very moderate drinker and on special occasions, as teenagers, the children had been allowed a small glass of wine and lemonade with a meal. Interestingly, the other three are now quite ambivalent about wine or any kind of alcohol and rarely take any.

But in his early twenties, James probably associated drinking with masculine adulthood and would sneak a glass of wine when nobody was around.

I remember being very angry with him on one occasion. David was out and James was watching television so I slipped across the road very briefly to see a neighbour who was ill. When I came back I found James, stretched out in his father's reclining chair, pipe in hand and a glass of wine on the mantelpiece!

Anger boiled up inside me and burst out in a flow of furious words. Typically James almost cowered, prepared to accept without question whatever I said or did. When the words finally stopped, I rushed off into the kitchen to try to control my quaking rage.

The anger at James for smoking and drinking (and enjoying it!) was nothing compared to my anger at myself for having left him alone to do it. I was also angry at the masculine lifestyle which was so appealing to him.

As these chaotic feelings slowly subsided, I began to see things differently. Wasn't James only doing exactly what he'd seen his father do night after night? Maybe he was even pretending to *be* his Dad! Then I realised that, if it *had* been his Dad I'd found in exactly the same circumstances, I would neither have felt nor said a thing!

I went slowly back into the living room. James was still sitting there. He looked at me apprehensively. I went and put my arms around him.

"Sorry James," I said. "I shouldn't have gone off at you like that. But I don't want you to be smoking and drinking."

He relaxed and smiled, patting me. "That's all right Mum." (James forgives immediately. And he never bears a grudge. If only I could be more like him!)

We went on to talk about the smoking and drinking, but in a more relaxed and constructive way. It would obviously be something to pray about.

But once he was away from home and had access to money for the first time, he began to experiment on his own in the local pubs.

More and more often, he began to withdraw money from his Post Office account and spend it on drink and fruit machines. He might set out with as much as £20 and not go home until he had spent every last penny. And because he was not living with us, he could do it without our knowing anything about it! Sometimes I only found out much later, when he would confess - or we would see the scars!

I talked to him of course, pointing out the dangers and the futility of excessive drinking. I tried to suggest alternatives which he would enjoy. We read Bible verses together which warn about the foolishness of drinking too much. And he always agreed with me. But nothing changed.

At times he seemed compelled to drink. One Saturday morning he came to see us. By this time we had sold Pitneil and moved to a small cottage on the sea front at Cowie, near Stonehaven, just half an hour's walk from James' home. It was a sunny day and we decided to go for a drive together. On the way back, James asked to be dropped off in the town to pick up films from the chemist. He said he would walk along to us for lunch.

But he never appeared. We waited and waited, finally ate our own lunch and waited some more. Then David set out on a search through various pubs and finally tracked him down, still drinking, and fit only to be taken home to bed.

We were at our wits end. What more could we do? We felt impotent. David tried a different approach - he went to all James' regular pubs and spoke to the barmen, asking them to mix his drinks with plenty of lemonade and to discourage him from spending too much on the bandits.

We asked the social helpers to withhold his money, but they said they were not able to do this. Nor, they pointed out, were we! I discovered to my horror that, legally, James was in charge of himself, and his finances.

"So," I said to the Social Worker in charge, "if James continues to drink and gamble, won't anyone *ever* step in to prevent him? Even if he becomes an alcoholic?"

I felt overwhelmingly angry that such a system

could have evolved without our realising it.

The Social Worker agreed to see what could be arranged. I continued to feel frustrated. I prayed - but I also spent sleepless hours going over arguments in my mind.

James had proved that he needed so little help - but he obviously still needed *some*. Possibly he always would. To me it seemed a permanent part of his handicap that he could not handle having access to money *and* the opportunity to drink. How could I just sit back and let him destroy himself?

Into this situation stepped the Community Nurse with a plan to give James special counselling through a course for people with alcohol problems. It had to be undertaken with the aid of a third party, and James chose me as his helper. Basically it involved working out a set of drinking rules, making certain promises and keeping a drinking record.

I was not too hopeful. Hadn't I been telling him these same rules and warning him of the same dangers? But I was glad of any help and willing to try anything. If the Community Nurse could succeed where I had failed, great!

The course recommended control rather than abstinence as being the wiser and more realistic aim. In our society there is a kind of sociability and acceptance to be found in local pubs which, unfortunately, does not seem to be available anywhere else. Perhaps James needed this social element. But in these situations James was most vulnerable, especially if he had money in his pocket - or friends at the bar. Incredibly, hotels are the venues where social activities organised by the SSMH take place, and they have been the scene of some of James' lapses.

James co-operated with the Nurse and worked his way through the whole course, which took several months. Where one of the agreed aims was for him to have two drink-free days a week, he would usually manage four or five. But where his recommended upper limit was four units (two pints) James would regularly break it by one extra pint.

To encourage him to keep his rules, the course recommended a system of frequent small rewards for staying within the limits. James rarely managed to qualify for any of these but we did work out one major reward for several months of good behaviour ... a continental holiday!

In spring 1991 James and I went on a six day coach tour of the Dutch bulbfields. We had a wonderful time, when he proved again what a great companion he could be. Thoughtful and caring, appreciative of the beautiful flowers and plants which we saw and photographed, he was readily accepted by the other members of the coach party and he thoroughly enjoyed the light-hearted evening activities in our hotel - without once over-indulging.

Since then his 'off-the-rails' drinking sprees have become less frequent. He still finds that the only way to achieve this is to ration himself strictly to taking only about three pounds when he goes out.

Obviously this will be an on-going point of concern. But even I, with my earlier scepticism, can see he is making progress ... if slowly.

CHAPTER 10

Hope For The Future

If you met James on the street in Stonehaven today, you'd see a slim-built, young man, striding along with characteristic loping gait, intent on where he's going. He'd be wearing an anorak and neatly pressed trousers, with a tweed cap hiding his receding hairline.

If you stopped to ask him the way, he would possibly direct you, but he'd be much more likely to go with you to be sure you arrived safely. And along the way, you'd notice that he was greeted by name by many local people.

Unfortunately, a casual encounter would not enable you to realise what a sensitive and deeply caring person he is.

Perhaps not surprisingly, this is most evident in his relationships with the family: especially his sisters and his nine nieces and nephews. As each baby arrived he knitted or stitched a soft toy for it - black and red golliwogs, brown rabbits and even a pink pig! And whenever any of the grandchildren visit us, Uncle James can be counted on as a very versatile, willing and fun-loving playmate.

Paul and his family live in Stonehaven so we see them regularly. But both Helen and Alison married in 1983 and went to live in Israel and Madrid respectively. James has been with us to visit both of them in their homes and when they occasionally manage to come to Scotland, he always wants to be part of the welcoming party at the airport.

He was especially glad to see Helen and her three children in February 1991 when they returned home for the duration of the Gulf War. He had not seen her since she was widowed the year before, and he hugged her hard. Though he could never put his feelings into words, he shows them in his actions.

So what of his future?

In 1991 James completed a course at a College in Aberdeen, travelling there by public transport with five other trainees. The aim of the course was to improve communication skills.

I never imagined that the Lord would dip into the coffers of the European Economic Community for James' benefit, but the EEC are, in fact, funding a follow-up to this course which James and others will attend for a further two years. The aim is to equip mentally handicapped adults for full-time employment, and actual work experience will be included in their schedule.

Every year James has a Review, attended by everyone connected with him from the Centre and Social Work Department, along with James and myself. It has been gratifying to see the progress he has made in response to the help he has been given by the team at Forest View.

In areas where I doubted whether he would ever change, such as his drinking and personal hygiene, he has made definite progress - though he still needs the support and promptings of his Homemaker. His work skills have also improved. He is still developing.

Personally I would hope that he will be able to live in the present Group home for a long time to come. I know that is where he wants to be. Even though he comes to stay with us for a week or two occasionally, he always wants to go back there to live. He values his independence.

David and I are both very grateful for all that has been done for James by the people who work for Grampian region, but my trust can never be in any man-devised system. They are just too liable to change and human error.

''James must be a worry for you.'' Many people have said this to me at different times in the past. And, taking into account the fact that we are getting older and James still has problems, I can understand their reasoning.

But I feel such people are leaving God out of their reckoning. James has known and loved the Lord Jesus for many years and he still reads his Bible faithfully, without prompting, every night, with the help of Scripture Union Quest Notes. Indeed, I am sure it is this habit of daily reading which has kept alive not only his faith but his reading skills.

When Dr. Billy Graham visited Aberdeen in 1991, James went forward to re-dedicate his life to Jesus. I believe Jesus will honour this commitment.

I also believe that James' life story to date shows that God has always had a concern for him. Maybe he has a plan and purpose beyond anything we can see or imagine. Isn't it the weak ones of this world who most clearly show his glory? Isn't it *we* who decide if people like James are to be our 'trials' or our sources of joy?

So although, as St. Paul reminds us in his second letter to the church at Corinth 'we are handicapped on all sides ... we are never frustrated (well, only sometimes!) we are puzzled, but never in despair' because 'we never have to stand it alone.' As he promised, God is with us ... in *everything*!

He has lovingly led, guided and provided for us

all throughout the years. And we know he is the same yesterday, today and forever. So it is to him that I entrust the future, for myself and for James - for our time in this world and for eternity.